THE MAGIC STONE

AND OTHER STORIES FOR
☐ THE FAITH JOURNEY ☐

By

James L. Henderschedt

Resource Publications, Inc.
160 E. Virginia Street, Suite 290
San Jose, CA 95112

Editorial director: Kenneth Guentert
Production editor: Elizabeth J. Asborno
Cover design and production: Ron Niewald

Library of Congress Cataloging-in-Publication Data
Henderschedt, James L., 1936-
 The magic stone.

 1. Christian fiction, American. I. Title.
PS3558.E4797M3 1988 813'.54 88-4367
ISBN 0-89390-116-4

5 4 3 2 1

Some of these stories originally appeared in Celebration *magazine.*

Table of Contents

These stories are dedicated with love to my partner in life, Betty, who has always encouraged the child in me to come out and play; and to my children, John, Beth, and Thomas, who reminded me through their own hunger for stories how important stories are.

Introduction

I have spent a lifetime answering forms all of which want to know my date of birth. I have become so accustomed to the question that it came as a complete surprise when I was asked recently when I experienced my birth trauma. To be sure, the natural birth process is traumatic for both mother and child. Even if the birthing is "easy," there can probably be nothing as rude as being introduced into this world with a sharp smack on a bare bottom. As barbarian as this may seem, that traumatic experience can make the difference between life and death.

Our existence is made up of a number of "birth" experiences all of which involve one kind of trauma or other. Each new beginning is a birth in itself. Baptism, the first day of school, one's wedding day, the death of a spouse are but a few examples that can be called a new beginning or the birthing of a new experience. You, the reader, can supply your own ideas about the traumas each one of these have and those you would add to the list.

We cannot ignore the birth trauma of one's spiritual life. At close evaluation our spirituality is not one continuous and unbroken line, but it is a series of beginnings, of birthings, that fuse together to make up what one may call their "spiritual journey." These too have their own kinds of traumatic experiences, some of which may cause us to tremble while others contain the exhileration of the mountaintop experience.

As we progress on our spiritual journey, we stop for a bit to wrestle with issues. When confronted by the cross of Jesus Christ, one may wonder what it means to be saved. A portion of Scripture may make us wonder about the spiritual dimension of loneliness. And not only do we explore these doctrinal puzzles, but we also try get our own lives into focus. When did the church become the people of God? None of these issues are easy to deal with, nor would we all agree unanimously with the answers that would be offered. Nevertheless, if we are to continue on our journey we will have to face them as St. George had to face the dragon.

Some of the wrestling I have done has taken its expression in the form of stories. Though they all may seem like fiction, they grow out of honest struggle with what it means to be here in God's kingdom at this particular time. They reflect those painful moments, those awkward moments, those joyful moments, those turbulent moments when my faith became the grist for the mill of spiritual struggle. These stories have not been easy for me to write simply because I had to relearn the meaning of the word "story."

Early in my childhood, my mother warned me that she did not want me to tell any "stories." In this context she meant a lie or a fib. Later, "story" became that special moment when I would transport my children into a land of pretend or excite their imaginations to live in a time when small shepherd boys slew giants with slingshots and foolish people built houses on sand.

Recently, however, my understanding of story took another turn. It happened when I allowed the child in me that was struggling against an adult world to emerge and discover that through stories common experiences can be shared; through stories we can walk side by side on the road of faith and find strength, hope, and joy in our common bond through Jesus Christ. Yes, even through stories that come close to being ridiculous, we can discover what it means to be a child in God's realm.

These stories are special moments for me. They are devotional, soul wrenching, spirit lifting, living and reliving of experiences that have been a part of my, and probably your, spiritual life birth trauma. They reflect those dark and lonely nights when I stood by the side of Nicodemus and said, "Yes, Lord, what must I do to inherit eternal life?" Through eyes that are warm and understanding, Jesus speaks those words of trauma: "You must be born again."

It is my prayer that these stories, which are my moments of theological reflection, will empower you to skillfully and seriously play with the images that the Word of God plants in your heart. But, more than that, I pray that these stories will release your childlike imagination and creativity and allow you to play in the theological sandbox of meditative reflection.

Although each story can stand by itself and can be read for personal enjoyment and/or growth, they can also be used in group settings such as retreats, workshops, Christian education classes, and koinonia gatherings. For those who would like to use them on a particular Sunday, or Feast day, references are included that identify those Sundays in the church year when each story could best be used.

I need to give special thanks to many of my partners who have listened to, read, and used these stories. Especially do I thank the Rev. Dr. Thomas Ridenhour, the Rev. Dr. Richard Thulin, the Rev. Dr. Donald Deffner, the Rev. Dr. Robert Hughes, Fr. Ed Hays, and Fr. Martin Bell, all of whom have touched my life in a special way and encouraged and inspired me to write and publish these stories. Lastly, a very special word of thanks to Sherry Deal, who so diligently and faithfully not only typed, corrected, and edited this manuscript, but who also allowed the child in her to respond to these stories and encouraged me to share them with you.

Sylvia's Lament

Theme: pride; use of God's gifts; priorities
Scripture: Jn 15:25; Rom 12:6-8
Feast: 15th Sunday after Pentecost (C cycle)

Sylvia stepped back to better survey her latest creation. First she cocked her head to the left, then to
the right. "Not bad," she said, knowing fully well
that only she would hear her own critique. "No,
not bad, if I must say so myself."

Sylvia had worked long and hard on this project. It
had to be just right. Sometimes she toiled so hard
that she had to stop and wipe the perspiration from
her brow. That was no easy matter for Sylvia, for you
see, Sylvia was a spider, and like all other spiders, she
had eight arms to choose from. At times, it was a
major decision simply to determine which arm she
would use. Concentrating hard, a message would be
sent to her tiny brain: "Third on the left." Almost in-
stantly that appendage would be put into action. Her
moment of satisfaction was her admiration of the web
she had just spun. It was a beauty! It was the most
perfect, geometrically accurate web ever constructed
in all of spiderdom.

Her ordeal started long before her web-spinning

began. She had to look carefully for the anchoring supports to which she would attach the silken threads. They had to be the right distance apart and strong enough to withstand the wind and the rain. But most of all, the web had to be constructed where it would be seen and admired.

After a diligent search, Sylvia finally decided to use the space between the railing on the human's porch. They met all of the qualifications. They were sturdy, made out of well-seasoned 2 x 4's, and offered her everything she needed for her web. But best of all, it would certainly be noticed. How excited Sylvia became thinking that the human, the crown of God's creation, would notice and admire her work of art. She would be the pride of the whole spider kingdom.

Now the job was done and she was very pleased ... and tired. Through the complex lenses of her eyes, she noticed that the sun was starting to set. The time for a well-deserved rest was at hand. Her miniscule heart beat rapidly just thinking how beautiful her web would look in the morning with the dew hanging like crystal baubles on the near invisible threads. Slowly she made her way around the perimeter of the web, making sure all of the anchor points were secure. She mended a small tear in one of the cross-strands and then settled down for an evening of peace and quiet. Her eyes started to close as she thought of all the uses her new web would have.

Suddenly her eyes opened wide. "Oh no!" she shouted out loud. "I forgot — a web is used for catching flying bugs and moths. If they get tangled in my web, they will destroy it! I can't let that happen! I've worked too hard on this web!"

So, Sylvia began her long vigil that night. She made all kinds of noises to scare away all of the flying insects that might fly too near her web.

"Beware," she called out, "there is a hungry spider here that will catch you in her web and eat you."

Often she heard the buzz of the wings of a fly or the fluttering of a moth turn away at the sound of her warning. Everything went well that evening; that is, until the human turned on the powerful porchlights.

"Turn off that stupid light," she commanded.

The lights began to attract a whole squadron of flying things. Of course, the human could not hear the frantic cries. Human hearing is not tuned in to the smaller sounds of nature. Sylvia ran from one strand to another, screaming, waving her legs, which we have already noted was not easy for her to do. As each insect approached her web, she went into a panic state, and she ran and shouted all the more.

It seemed almost an eternity, but the light was finally extinguished. Sylvia did not rest much that night. She kept constant guard to protect her web. It had to be preserved. She still hadn't heard anyone tell her how nice it was, and she would never be able to make another like it.

Dawn finally came. Sylvia was finally exhausted. She hadn't slept a wink. In fact, she was so tired that she did not notice the dew drops clinging to the web, glistening, reflecting the colors of the spectrum like miniature prisms. All of creation was still ... until all hell broke loose. The silence was shattered by the call of the abusive bluejay. Every day that bird bullied anything it knew would not fight back. "That crazy bird," Sylvia thought to herself. She had watched it almost every morning that summer. It liked to swoop down and scare smaller creatures. One of its favorite stunts was to fly at breakneck speed between the rails of the porch and then pull up just before it hit. "Oh my God!" Sylvia was filled with terror. "That idiot with wings is going to destroy my web." Sylvia thought and thought of ways she could keep the jay away. Then an idea came to her. She had watched as the human made a likeness of himself to put in the garden and scare away the birds. A "scarecrow" he called it. "I'll make me a 'scare jay.'" High above her on the branch of a tree, she spied a huge caterpillar slowly lumbering along. Carefully, Sylvia crept up behind her unsuspecting victim. At the right moment, she attacked, injecting her poison into the surprised larva and then waiting until the quivering of life ceased. It was almost instantaneous. The victim was caught off guard and died quickly and relatively painlessly. Laboring under the weight of the huge burden, Sylvia tugged the corpse until she could place it on the edge of her web. She spun a darkened thread around the body and inserted some twigs.

"There," she said, when she finished her job. "It looks even scary to me. Now, let's see if it will work."

Sure enough, the jay was about to make one of its kamikaze runs through the rails. It climbed high in the air, paused for a moment, and made a steep, blinding dive. It was almost at the point of no return when it saw the big, black, ugly thing sitting right in its path. The jay did not want to tangle with that critter.

Sylvia waited for the recognition she expected from the human. But it never came. How heartbroken she was the first time he stepped out on the porch. She picked herself up, even smiled half with embarrassment, thinking of how proud she would be of herself. But her smile vanished as he walked on by without so much as a sign that he even noticed that the web was there.

"Hey dummy!" Sylvia shouted as loudly as she could, "can't you see my web? Aren't you even going to stop and look at it?"

He didn't, and Sylvia was hurt.

"Damn it all anyway!" she cried as she kicked one of the supporting strands of the web. The kick sent the whole web into a shivering fit, putting a tremendous strain on the anchor points. Sylvia realized her mistake and make a mental note never to kick the web again. She didn't want to damage the web, even if others didn't appreciate it.

Well, the hours passed into days and the days into weeks, and Sylvia kept her constant watch over her web. It stayed intact. Whenever a strand tore, Sylvia hastened to make the repair. But as time went on, Sylvia became weaker and weaker. A web is the way a spider catches its food. All this time that Sylvia was busy preserving her web, she was not eating. To catch a fly or moth for food meant she that must use the strands of her web to tie the victim up, and we know that Sylvia would not do that. Her web was too important to her.

One day Sylvia awoke from a fitful nap. "Oh no," she fretted. "I fell asleep. Did anything happen to my web? I've got to check it and see."

In fact, nothing did happen to her web. But when Sylvia went to make the inspection, she found that she was too weak to move. Then she knew that death was near.

As each minute passed, so did Sylvia's strength. Slowly, with much great effort, she was able to crawl to the outer edge of her web and then onto one of the railings that served as an anchor for her web. She wanted to take one last look at her web.

"Was it worth it?" she asked herself.

Just before her eyes closed for the last time, she took her final look at her perfect web. At that moment a blue blur swooped between the railings of the porch, completely erasing any signs that the most beautiful, the most geometrically perfect web ever existed. The very last thing Sylvia saw before she died was the human, standing in the doorway, laughing at the crazy bird.

Lord, you have not passed me by but have bestowed on me and all your children gifts beyond measure. Preserve me from the selfish pride that would clench these gifts in a tight fist, and open my hands, heart, and mind to be generous in the sharing of these blessings you give so lavishly.

The Magic Stone

Theme: finding treasures in unexpected places
Scripture: Mt 13:44
Feast: tenth Sunday after Pentecost (A cycle)

Inch by inch, my eyes surveyed the ground in front of me. "Don't look at the soil," my uncle had told me years before, "look at the stones. Look at each of them, one at a time. Pick them up. Rub the dirt off of them. Use your walking stick to turn over the small clumps of ground. Look for the telltale signs: a point sticking up out of the earth, a recognizable profile, a flat end. Go slow. The surprise awaits you."

The leaves from the tall stalks of field corn brushed against my face. Nearby, three rows to my left and a few paces behind me, I could hear my uncle as he expertly used his walking stick as an extension of his arm.

"Will I find it?" I wondered half aloud. So many years of looking with nothing to show for it. How many stones did I pick up, only to cast them to the side. "Useless, only a rock." How many times did my heart beat rapidly within my breast as I bent over to pick up what I had hoped was the object of my search?

This day was like all the others. I wanted to quit a number of times, but my uncle urged me on with words of encouragement. "Keep on looking," he said. "You'll find it!"

Almost beneath my feet, a small triangular piece of stone protruded at a drunken angle. I dug it out and began to clean off the dirt with my thumb. Slowly, a form began to take shape. My hands started to tremble. Tears of joy and excitement filled my eyes. I wanted to call out to my uncle, but all that came out was a strangulated croak — for I held in my hand the magic stone!

When I looked up I found that I was no longer standing in a cornfield. The power of the stone had taken effect. I was standing in a village. Women were busy making the evening meal over open fires. Dogs chased young children at play, barking and nipping at the heels of the slower, tinier tots. Young girls stood in a small group, giggling as they coyly watched the boys show off their budding strength in a mock wrestling match, knowing fully well that they were being observed. A handsome young man, his skin bronzed by the summer sun, stepped into the clearing with an animal slung over his shoulder. It would provide food for the village for a number of days. His wife came through the opening of their hut, holding a small baby who nursed greedily at her bare, full breast. In embarrassment I wanted to divert my eyes, but the smile on the faces of the proud parents would not let me look away. Filled with wonder and awe at being in another place and time, I slowly walked through the small gathering of hastily built huts. The aroma of the cooking food reminded me that I was hungry, but I dared not ask for food for fear that the spell would be broken. This was the moment for which I had waited so very, very long, and I wanted to savor every moment possible.

When I came to the edge of the village, near the rain-swollen creek, I came upon a young boy, about my age, sitting cross-legged on the ground. In one hand he held a small, black stone. In the other was a spike from a deer's antler, which he was using as a tool to break away small chips from the stone. I recognized with amazement that it was the stone I held in my hand.

The magic stone had brought me into the presence of the creator of the object of my long and diligent search.

I could not keep my silence any longer. The need for the completion of the bond of time filled me with a desire to bridge the dimension that separated us.

Just as I was ready to speak, I heard a voice call me, so faint it seemed to come from the future.

"Jimmy," the voice called over and over again. "Jimmy, Jimmy."

Slowly I came back, aware of the rustling of the corn leaves around me. At my side was my uncle. He was holding my hand, in which I held the magic stone.

"Jimmy," he said, "you found it. It is beautiful. That is the most perfect arrowhead that was ever found in this field. I am very proud of you and happy for you."

Yes, to my uncle, I did find a near-perfect arrowhead. He didn't know, nor did anyone else know; only you and I know it wasn't just an arrowhead. It was *the magic stone.*

Your whole kingdom and creation is an open field, O Lord, in which is buried treasure. These treasures are found in people, places, and events. Open me to such treasures as a child's smile, the fragrance of a rose, a lover's kiss, a firefly's light, or the sparkling of a star. No greater possession can I have than that which is hidden around me.

Alice's Foot

Theme: God's adoption; special to God; God's child
Scripture: Phil 2:5-8
Feast: 19th Sunday after Pentecost (A cycle); Passion Sunday (A, B, C cycles); fifth Sunday of Lent (C cycle)

Alice had been through this many times before. She couldn't remember how often her hopes were raised only to have them dashed to the floor. The pattern was always the same. First, there was the call to leave the dorm room she shared with others at the orphanage. Then there was the wait outside of the superintendent's office, listening to the muffled voices behind the closed door discussing her. Words like "slow" and "difficult" came through often. Finally, there was the inch-by-inch scrutiny that made her feel more like a specimen under a microscope than the homeless, parentless girl that she was. She hated the women who looked at her the way they did a piece of meat hanging in the butcher's shop. And they all smelled like lilacs and Alice hated lilacs.

Bad memories came back as she now stood under the searching stares of the young man and woman in front of her. She remembered how one lady wouldn't even look at her after she saw how poorly her dress fit. Another didn't want to have anything to do with her because she stuttered and the servants would only laugh at her. Yet another was afraid that Alice's club foot would make her too clumsy to be a good serving girl. Tears welled up when she remembered how she was once slapped when she tripped and her hands brushed against the lilac-smelling woman's soft fur coat.

Alice felt very self-conscious in front of this couple. The woman's hair was soft and radiant, and Alice's was a tangled mass of knots. The woman's face was clean and glowing while Alice's was dirty and tear-stained. In vain, Alice tried to hide her misshapen foot behind the good one.

The pretty, young lady sat erect in front of Alice. The folds of her long dress reached neatly to the floor. Slowly, the tall, handsome man walked around Alice. At intervals he would stop, glance toward his wife and raise an eyebrow as a thin smile barely traced his lips. He circled Alice a couple of times and then went to his wife's side. Not a word was spoken as they looked deep into one another's eyes for the longest time. Finally, he turned to the superintendent, who sat behind his mahogany desk, and said, "Yes, she's the one. We would like to have her."

The superintendent shook his head in disbelief.

Alice was stunned. "Y-y-you m-m-mean y-y-you want me t-t-to b-b-be your s-s-serving g-g-girl?" she asked.

"No, Alice," the pretty lade said. "We want you to be our daughter."

Alice could not believe what she heard. No-one had ever said that to her before. Often she had dreamed about what it would be like having a mother and father and a home.

"It can't be true," she said to herself. She wanted them to tell her again.

"You really want me to be your daughter — to live with you in your house?" Alice wasn't even aware she didn't stammer a bit.

"Yes," the handsome man said. "We've never had any

children. My wife and I have so much love to give, and we want to give that love to you. We want you to be happy."

"But why me?" Alice asked, remembering the many times she was turned down by the others.

The pretty lady stood up and smiled at Alice. Slowly she reached down and lifted her floor-length skirt and revealed her own malformed foot. Softly, lovingly, and understandingly, she said to Alice, "Today we want you to be our child. Please Alice, let us love you."

I'm not perfect, Lord. None of us are. There is something we try to hide from you and others. We even begin to believe it when we think we are unlovable. But you have the last word with us. That word is "You are mine." You made us and we are yours. When lost, you saved us. So we can pray as Jesus taught, Our Father ...

The Day

Theme: the birth of Christ
Scripture: Lk 2:1-20
Feast: Christmas Eve or Christmas Day

The Kingdom was bustling with activity. Mordachi stepped through the doorway of his abode, stretching, blinking in the brilliant light of day. Rubbing the sleep from his eyes, he thought to himself, "Our God, things are busy out here. There is so much activity it is like a beehive in the middle of a pollen-gathering time.

"Hey," he called out to a neighbor who was hurrying by. "What's going on?"

"Mordachi, have you been sleeping again?" the neighbor responded. "I swear (if you will pardon the expression), all of eternity is going to pass you by and you will not even notice it."

Mordachi accepted the good-natured jibe. "Never mind with the smart-aleck stuff. Just tell me why everyone is running around."

Well, Mordachi," the neighbor said, "if you were sleeping you probably did not hear the news. Today is *The Day!*"

"How's that again?" Mordachi asked.

"It is *The Day*. It is finally here after so long a time waiting for it. And because it is *The Day*, none of us wants to miss it. We all want to be ready when it happens. I've got to go. See you around."

Mordachi turned to go back into his house. "It's *The Day*," he said half aloud with a sharp edge to his voice. "How many times have I heard that before? It's *The Day*. How I wish it would be true. So many times the news went out, only *The Day* never came. Things are the same as they always were, if not worse, really."

Mordachi's concern was real and legitimate. *The Day* was announced or anticipated a number of times before, but nothing changed. Things were still as bad as before. In some parts of the world, people had so much food that they got fat by overeating, but elsewhere there was no food. Mordachi had seen people so thin, their skin so dry and brittle, that they resembled leaves that fell from trees in October and blown away by the slightest gust of wind.

He had known *The Day* had not come when he observed how deep and intense was the hatred and intolerance of people toward each other. Even within families people were driving themselves apart by their inability to find love for and in the other person.

And then there was life, or to be specific, the lack of concern for it. Life was so cheap. It was taken almost without a second thought. And oh, how his heart ached as he observed how clever man thought he was as he discovered newer and more efficient ways of taking life from others. No, *The Day*, though promised, had never come.

Mordachi stood looking out of the single window of his sparsely furnished room. His eyes filled with tears as he watched his fellow citizens excitedly hurry about in preparation for and in anticipation of the coming of *The Day*. Would they be hurt? Would they be disappointed again?

"No!" he shouted, slamming his fist down in his hand. "I won't let it happen. This time I'll be sure. I'll ask Him. I will go directly to the One."

Mordachi set off from his house, not without fear and trembling. You just did not go to the One unless your business was serious. It certainly was to Mordachi, but he was not sure the One would agree.

He moved with determination, brushing past those who were hurrying and scurrying in expectation of the great celebration. Up and up he moved as he ascended on high to the presence of the One.

Finally, Mordachi stood outside the place of the presence. He was always amazed at how humble the place was for such a wise and powerful being. It was not at all unlike the place where Mordachi dwelt — small, but sufficient; sparse, but ample; unpretentious, but esthetic.

With trembling hand Mordachi pushed open the door. Inside the bright room, the One sat in the middle of the floor. He was veiled, as usual, in mystery.

Mordachi approached the One and sat in front of him cross-legged on the floor. He felt the eyes of the One rest upon him. It should have been a frightening sensation, but it was not. Mordachi felt a kind of fatherly compassion as the One waited patiently for him to state the purpose of his visit.

Taking a deep breath, Mordachi asked with a sense of urgency and concern, "Is this *The Day?*"

The One smiled (at least it seemed as though He did to Mordachi) and held up his hand.

What happened then caused the whole universe to tremble. A sudden hush came over all that was, that is, and that ever will be. For one brief moment, all that is bad and evil and inhumane and malevolent and wrong came to a stop. The tools of war ceased rolling and the sin of inhumanity halted. The wind stopped its roaring; the sea its crashing; earthquakes their trembling; floods their flowing. And over the deafening silence prevailed but one sound. It was the cry of a newborn infant.

A great shout was heard from the whole Kingdom. Stars danced in the sky and in the corner of the eyes of the One glistened tears as clear and brilliant as the most perfect diamonds. In the softest of whispers, the One said, "Yes, Mordachi, this is *The Day*."

Mordachi sprang to his feet and ran out of the presence of the One without so much as a "good-bye" or "thank you." He could hardly believe it. Finally, after so many millennia of waiting, it had come.

All of the beings in the Kingdom hurried to one very tiny spot in the universe where they could see that which made *The Day* so special. They stopped over a small, remote village on the planet Earth. Mordachi pushed and stretched and jostled those in his way, but he could not see. There were so many of them.

Looking to the side, Mordachi saw a small group of men, shepherds they were called, cringing in fear of the heavenly spectacle. He was moved to compassion by their awe and trembling.

Mordachi went to them and said in a voice so filled with joy that even he was surprised by it, "Do not be afraid. This is *The Day!* You have born to you a savior. He is Christ ... the Lord!"

At that, the entire host of heaven raised their voices in an anthem so mighty and powerful that it echoed to the uppermost parts of the whole of creation ... an anthem so sweet that the One stood in reverence and blended his own voice with that of the rest ... an anthem so filled with love that never again will anything be the same:

"GLORY TO GOD IN THE HIGHEST AND ON EARTH PEACE ..."

I blend my voice with those of your angels and sing, Glory to God. On that night most holy, you gave to all the Prince of Peace. May there always be a place in us for the Word to become flesh.

Dawn's Early Light (A Sequel)

Theme: Resurrection; Easter
Scripture: Mk 16:1-7
Feast: Easter

Thirty-three years," Mordachi thought to himself. "Thirty-three years since *The Day*." He remembered the excitement that ran wild throughout the Kingdom and his own skepticism. Sitting in the mysterious presence of the One seemed like only yesterday. He would never forget the beautiful sound of the birthing cry. And then there were his own words to the frightened shepherds, "Don't be afraid. A son is born to you today and he is Christ the Lord."

Now a generation had passed and the years had not been kind. That Special Child was all that the Wise Ones of the Kingdom had said he would be. He loved those who were unlovable; brought joy to the sorrowful; gave hope to the hopeless, healing to the sick, sanity to the possessed, and life to the dying.

He did so many special things. In the wilderness he went nose to nose and toe to toe with Old Scratch and wupped him. He tamed the wild-eyed demoniac of Gerazine. In the midst of a storm that frightened seasoned sailors, he faced the wind and angry sea and brought everything under control.

"But, what was the use?" Mordachi shouted out loud as he finished packing his bag.

Tears streamed down his cheeks as the events of the past days came back. Try as he might, he could not block them from his mind. Everyone in the Kingdom knew all was not well. Though this Special Child did and said many good things, those in power refused to hear or understand. It finally came to the point where the religious leaders could cope only with his death, and they set out to plot against his life. Taking the life of someone so loved would not be easy. But they succeeded. Yes, they succeeded by feeding the greed of one of his followers. "Judas," Mordachi spat as though he just eaten something bitter.

Everyone in the Kingdom knew what was happening. Again the Wise Ones had foretold the destiny of this Child. No-one wanted to think about it. They put it out of their minds with the hopes that if they did not think about it, it wouldn't happen.

But it did. What sadness there was when they all watched helplessly as the Child prayed, "Father, if it is possible, let this cup pass from me." Mordachi even looked up the One, willing Him to intervene. But all He did was sadly hang his head as if helpless.

That was not the end of it. What followed made justice a travesty. The trial was a mockery. The temple rulers had already determined his guilt and punishment. The political governors were too cowardly to intervene. Even the people were seduced into calling for his end.

And then there came the verdict: death by crucifixion. Mordachi shivered, remembering the shameful treatment and the torturous walk to that hill overlooking Jerusalem's garbage dump, carrying the heavy crossbar to which his hands would be nailed.

Mordachi placed his hands over his ears as he heard once again the thunderous blow of the hammer that drove the metal spikes into the wrists and feet of that Special Child. A deep moaning welled up in the Kingdom, clouds gathered, and in the place where there is no darkness, darkness prevailed. Once again Mordachi had lifted his eyes to the One, only to see Him with his face in his hands and his shoulders trembling with weeping as no-one has ever wept before.

Well, Mordachi had had it! That was the last straw! First there were all of the false appearances of *The Day*. Now, after it really happened, this terrible event was allowed to take place. There was no hope for anyone. This whole idea about a Holy Nation, a Royal Priesthood, a New Jerusalem was a lot of idle talk. The hope of anything good died with the death rattle of the Special Child nailed on a cross. Mordachi was going to leave the Kingdom. He did not want to have any part of this. It was all a cruel hoax.

He finished packing his modest possessions, just enough to fill a backpack, looked around his abode for the last time, and walked out, closing and locking the door behind him. It was still dark. A strange peace, a quietness hung over the Kingdom. It was just like what happens after an early morning spring rain. "Another false sense of security," Mordachi said just loud enough for himself to hear.

Slowly, Mordachi walked away, shifting his backpack so that it would ride comfortably as he walked. Just once he turned around, filled with sadness as he thought of what could have been and somewhat angry at what was.

Out of respect he decided to stop by the grave in which the dead body of the Special Child was placed. It was the least he could do. He doubted if anyone else in the Kingdom would show this much respect.

The early morning air was cool. On the horizon the first hint of the dawn started to glow. Mordachi stood in front of the huge, round stone that covered the mouth of the burial tomb. He lowered his eyes to offer his prayer of lament. But, while he was praying, Mordachi sensed a slight trembling in the ground beneath his feet. Startled, he looked up and saw the stone (which resembled a mill's grinding wheel) slowly roll back.

"It cannot be," Mordachi thought as he stood amazed at what he saw. No-one was pushing the stone; it was rolling back on its own.

Mordachi wanted to run away from this situation. He had a strange sense of dread mingled with curiosity.

Suddenly, a light brighter than a thousand suns burst forth from the dark maw of the grave. Mordachi was stunned as though struck on the back of his head. He did not understand what was happening.

He did not know how much time had passed. He slowly regained his senses as he felt a slight pressure on his left shoulder. It felt like someone's hand was resting there. He looked, squinting through the blinding light. Mordachi couldn't believe what he saw. There, smiling at him with the biggest, warmest, most beautiful smile was the Special Child.

The Special Child squeezed the shoulder of Mordachi, looked deeply into his eyes, and then walked off in the direction of the city.

Mordachi, with tears of joy streaming down his cheeks, began to laugh and dance. Now he *knew*. Now he *understood*. It wasn't the end. It was just the beginning.

Mordachi climbed to the top of the round stone and sat on it, laughing, singing, swinging his legs like a little child sitting in a chair too big for him.

"Up from the grave he arose," he sang with all his might. "The powers of death take flight. The gift of life is ours to have. The wrong of sin is now made right."

Once, Mordachi saw the shadow of Satan lurking behind the trees. Laughing like a silly child, Mordachi stuck out his tongue, put his thumbs in his ears, wiggled his fingers, and called out, "Take that Ol' Scratch. You've met your match. It's all over for you."

What a happy day! What a glorious day.

Then he heard footsteps. Some women carrying spices and cloth strips for burial approached. They were startled at what they saw: the open grave and a young man dressed in white sitting on the stone, singing and swinging his legs.

They slowly went near. Mordachi jumped down from his perch. He was filled with so much happiness, he felt like he would burst.

"Where is he?" the women asked.

Mordachi, with the gentle rays of dawn's early light reflecting his own joy, said, "This Jesus whom you seek is not here. He is risen. He who was dead is alive just as he told you he would be. Go back and tell the rest what you have seen and heard and that he going on before you and will meet you in Galilee. Christ is risen. He is risen indeed!"

My heart leaps for joy. My lips sing your praise. You live as you have promised. The grave is empty, the powers of death have been scattered, the bondage of Satan is broken. You are among the living. You live to bring life to an arid and barren existence. For all of this I praise your holy name.

The Woodcarver's Gift

Theme: God's gifts; gift giving; God's grace
Scripture: Mt 20:1-16
Feast: 18th Sunday after Pentecost (A cycle)

O nce upon a time, in a land long ago and far away, there lived a woodcarver. He was a fine craftsman, and people came from far and near to see his carvings. He was loved by all, especially the children of the village. They would come to watch, their button noses pressed against the glass of the shop's window.

He was a happy man. He had everything he needed. But most important of all he had two very near and dear friends, the tailor and the teacher, and a lovely niece who cared for him.

But for all he had, he was not satisfied. He had a dream. He wanted to carve a masterpiece. The wood had to be special, so for many years he sought the perfect piece. Finally, one day, he found it. Its texture was just right; the color subtle; the grain seemed to suggest the majesty that was locked up in his imagination.

One night, at a meal he was sharing with his niece and friends, the carver shared his dream. Immediately the others were caught up in the dream too. "Oh uncle," the niece said, "may I be the model?"

The tailor, hardly able to contain his enthusiasm, said, "I'll make a special robe. It will be made of the finest material and it will drape in a way fit only for a queen."

"And I," added the teacher, "will teach your niece to think, look, and walk like a regal lady."

So they all went about their tasks. The niece modeled, the tailor made the robe, and the teacher taught, while the carver carved. Hours passed into days, days into weeks, weeks into months.

One day, months later, the niece, tailor, and teacher were invited to dine with the carver. The carving was complete, and it was time to see what was done. They were all excited that day. The tailor was so beside himself that he sewed two right arms onto the mayor's new ceremonial jacket. The teacher, unable to concentrate, dismissed school early that day. And the niece almost forgot to cook the potatoes.

Finally the evening came; the meal was a feast, the kind reserved for special days. The room was warm; the food hot; the wine mellow. And in the center of the room, bathed in the flickering light of the candles, stood the draped carving.

When the last dishes were cleared from the table and the wine glasses filled for the last time, the carver reverently walked up to the table upon which the carving stood. Adoringly he traced the outline of the figure on the outside of the drape. Tears began to well in his warm, blue eyes. He pulled at the cloth covering the carving, and the drape fell to the floor. There was an audible gasp. It seemed as though everyone stopped breathing. No-one ... nothing moved. Even the candles refused to flicker, but cast a steady ray upon the Madonna, the mother of Jesus.

"It's beautiful," whispered the niece.

"I thought I just saw the robe move," said the tailor with wonder.

"Such innocence is captured in her face," observed the teacher.

It was truly what the carver always wanted — a master-piece.

The carver faced his guests. "I have made a very important decision," he announced. "This carving is more than my imagination ever conceived. I feel as though my hands were guided by someone other than myself. I am going to give the carving to the village church."

The tailor began to sputter. "What?" he demanded. "Have you lost your senses? You can't do that. They will never appreciate it. Beside, I think the carving would look good in my shop window. The people will know what a fine tailor I am when they see how beautiful the robe is."

The teacher agreed that it should not go to the church. He suggested, however, that inasmuch as he had taught the niece the important facts about being a lady, the stat-ue ought to be in his classroom as a tribute to his excel-lent skill.

The niece began to cry. "Oh, uncle. I would so much like to have the robe the tailor made. You could sell the carving and buy the robe for me."

The carver's face became red with rage. Trying to gather his self-control, he said with a quavering voice, "It is true that each of you contributed something to my carving. But you offered it. I did not ask for it. It is also true that your contribution was important. But this is my creation. I made it and I will do with it as I please. It will go to the church."

And to the church it went. Now, you might think that this is a happy solution and that everyone ended up being pleased. But it is not the end, for you see, there was a divi-sion among the people of the congregation. On the one hand, there were those who wanted it in the church (though for the life of them they couldn't tell why). On the other hand, there were those who didn't want the carving of the Madonna in their church. "It makes us too much like them," they argued, meaning like the other group they were too afraid of being identified with, though they didn't know why they were afraid.

And so the woodcarver's gift created tension in the church. One group began preparing a place for the carving, while the other group looked for support to prevent it. The conflict became so severe that both sides, now taken to sitting on opposite sides of the aisle in church, decided to have the pastor settle the matter once and for all.

Now, the pastor was not a very effectual fellow. He never made a decision anyone ever thought was profound. His sermons cured insomnia. He was rather dull and slow of wit. The people tolerated him because the bishop promised someone better when this one was finally moved. Nevertheless, he was the pastor. And if someone did not like the decision, better to blame him instead of a friend or neighbor.

The time for the decision came. The church was full. Those in favor of the carving sat on the right side. Those against sat on the left. Little boys stuck their tongues out at one another while the girls giggled because they found the whole matter rather silly.

The pastor stood in front of the carving for a long time. Most people thought he was meditating. But really, he was frightened because he didn't have the faintest notion of what to say.

A hush drew over the congregation as he finally ascended the steps to the pulpit. Nervously, he cleared his throat. "Brothers and sisters in Christ," his voice cracked, "there are some among you who oppose placing this carving in our church because you feel it is wrong to pray to statues. You are right for so thinking."

Smiles appeared on the faces of everyone on the left side of the church.

"And some of you are in favor of placing it here because it is a thing of beauty, and you are also right."

Now everyone on the right side was smiling. In fact, everyone was smiling. But suddenly, they realized a decision had not been made. Again, the pastor cleared his throat and said, "Now I want to tell all of you why you are wrong."

All smiles vanished.

"As I gazed upon this workmanship," he continued, "I saw a beautiful young woman. It reminded me that Jesus, the Word of God, became flesh, was born of a woman, and lived a life like yours and mine. He lived. He died as we all do and shall. He was a living, human being. That is the miracle of the Incarnation. But that is not all. This same Jesus rose from the dead and is offering all of us a new life, so that today as you and I live as his disciples and receive the bread and wine of Holy Communion, we become a part of that Incarnation as Christ becomes flesh in and through us. So, my friends, this carving is not an object of worship. It was not meant to be. It is an object of faith that reminds us and points us to the greater truth of salvation in Jesus Christ. Nor is it simply a work of art. It is more than that. It is a symbol of the creative power of the living God. This carving, a gift from our woodcarver, reminds me of God's greater gift. So, it shall have its place here among us in this church. Amen!"

As the pastor descended the stairs, he looked out and saw a miracle taking place. Hands of friendship were reaching across the aisle. Differences were put aside as, perhaps like never before, his people were one in Christ.

Well, not everyone agreed with him that day. The tailor still thought it should be in his shop window to advertise his skill. The teacher thought it ought to be in his classroom as a sign of his ability. The niece thought she should have the new robe. They didn't understand. And I guess that's okay too. For as the prophet once wrote: "Your thoughts are not my thoughts; neither are your ways my ways, says the Lord!"

Why am I jealous of my neighbor? You have made me a special person and endowed me with sufficient grace. I am a part of your family. Even the least is great in your eyes. Let me not be consumed by greed, but fill me with the splendor of your kingdom.

Leroy's First Flight

Theme: risk taking; surrendering to the Spirit
Scripture: Jn 3:6-8; 8:32
Feast: Trinity Sunday (B cycle)

Leroy was not all that unusual. He really wasn't the kind that would stick out in a crowd. In fact, in almost every way, he was ordinary. The only difference between Leroy and all the other ducks on the pond was that Leroy was afraid to fly.

It isn't that he never tried to fly. He did, a couple of times. He watched as all the other ducks started to flap their wings, then run like mad until they were actually running on the surface of the water. Then, just at the right moment, they would pull up their feet and *Presto!* they would be airborne.

Well, that looked like fun to Leroy, so he tried to mimic what he had observed. First, he started to pump his wings as fast as he could. Then he got his feet moving so that he was cruising at a respectable clip. Even Leroy was surprised when he felt his feet touching on top of the pond's smooth water. Next, he pulled up his feet — and plunged headfirst back into the pond. When he surfaced, he was coughing and sputtering. It was most humiliating to hear all the other ducks and geese laughing at him.

Out of the corner of his eye, he even saw his mother shake her head in disappointment.

You might think that would make Leroy give up flying, but it didn't! He tried again, one more time. However, to be on the safe side, he started on dry land. He wasn't going to chance another dunking, nor did he want to amuse the other denizens of the pond.

Now, takeoff from land involves much the same procedure, at least while you are still a novice and just learning how to fly. Once the wing muscles are developed and the technique is mastered, ducks can take off from a standing position. But since Leroy still had to do his first solo, he had to repeat the previous procedure. First the flapping of the wings, then running like crazy. Before he knew what was happening, Leroy was in the air. He was flying! And he flew right smack into a tree. Leroy make a terrible thud when he hit the ground.

He could tell that the other ducks were doing all they could to keep from rolling over and dunking themselves. He thought he detected a tear in the corner of his mother's eye — not because she felt sorry for him, but because she would be the laughing stock of the matron's club.

That did it for Leroy, though. No way was he going to chance it again. Not only was he afraid that he would never be able to live down his humiliation, but he also concluded that flying was dangerous. This meant that if Leroy wanted to get anywhere, he either had to swim or walk.

Now, when God made ducks, he obviously meant them to swim or fly. If you have ever seen the east end of a westbound duck, you know God did not have walking in mind when ducks were created.

Nevertheless, Leroy swam and walked — mostly swam. Anyone who visited the pond would not notice that Leroy didn't fly. Other ducks and geese were always swimming around, so Leroy looked right at home. But Leroy knew, and so did his mother and the other ducks.

Truthfully, it wasn't all that bad. Maybe his webbed feet were more shriveled than the others', but Leroy didn't mind. He was content to live with that small inconvenience. And that's how Leroy spent his summer — swimming and walking.

One day, however, Leroy began to notice a change. The air was getting cooler; leaves were falling from the trees; restlessness was stirring among all the ducks and geese. Leroy felt it too, but he didn't know what it meant. He asked an older member of the flock, who told Leroy that autumn was approaching and that all the ducks and geese were getting ready to fly south.

That was all Leroy needed to hear. His blood froze in his veins. No way was he going to fly south; yet he was being pulled by that strange feeling inside.

The time came when the ducks and geese began their yearly migration. At first, just a few took off — probably to scout for good resting places along the way. Then larger and larger groups left. They weren't quiet about it either.

But Leroy didn't budge.

Finally, the oldest member of the flock, the one who waited to see that all got off safely, saw that Leroy wasn't making his move. He swam to Leroy and told him that he needed to leave soon. It was going to get cold, and Leroy was too young to survive the harsh weather that was coming. If he didn't leave, Leroy would die.

"But I'm afraid," Leroy protested. He knew he had to go. There was only one thing he could do; he went to the wise, old member of the flock and asked, "Which way is south?"

The elder pointed with the tip feathers of his wing, and Leroy swam to the shore, waddled up onto dry land, and started to walk. Yes, that's right. Leroy decided to walk south.

You can imagine what a sight that was: a little, southbound duck walking down the center of the highway, following the double yellow line.

It was slow going, but Leroy didn't mind. If he was going to get to where he was supposed to be, he was going to have to walk there. And things did go pretty well for Leroy, until the traffic got heavy.

The cars had to slow down for him, and some drivers said some pretty nasty things to him. But Leroy didn't let that bother him. He had to get south, and he was determined to get there if it was the last thing he did — even if it had to be the slowest way.

We almost lost Leroy. One afternoon, a fully loaded eighteen-wheeler barreled down on Leroy and did not see him until the last moment. It was too late to stop. The driver swerved to avoid hitting the duck in the middle of the highway. He missed Leroy, but the turbulence caused by the passing truck rolled Leroy around a couple of times. He became a blur of feathers, webbed feet, and orange beak. When Leroy stopped rolling, he was dazed. He also lost his orientation and didn't know which way was south. Now his greatest fear was a reality. He wouldn't make it. He waddled to the side of the road, sat down, and started to cry. He didn't want to fly, and he didn't want to die. What was he to do? Which way was he to go?

Just then he heard something — something familiar. It was the honking of geese. A flock of the rear guard flew overhead, and Leroy's heart jumped for joy. Now he knew which way was south. He started to run (well, he called it running) in the direction the geese were flying. But just then, a strong gust of wind came along and hit Leroy head on. It knocked him off balance; he had to spread his wings to gain control, and when he did, another gust of wind lifted him off the ground. Leroy soared high into the air. Before he knew what was happening, Leroy looked down and saw the ground falling farther and farther away. Cars, buildings, people, the highway were all getting smaller and smaller.

"I'm flying!" he shouted. "I'm really flying!"

Hesitantly at first, he moved his outstretched wings.

He discovered he could control the direction, speed, even the altitude of his flight. He became braver and braver until finally he was flying with as much confidence as a duck can have on his first solo flight.

It wasn't long before he caught up with the geese he had seen. Ducks don't normally fly south with geese, but Leroy was so proud, he wanted to show someone that he was really flying. And the geese didn't mind either. In fact, it was a novel thing for them. Now they would have something to tell the flock when they arrived. Leroy was also anxious because he would have quite a story to tell his flock.

And they did!

Lord, you want me to spread my wings and fly. But I am afraid. Will others laugh at me if I do? Will I get off the ground and not be able to land? You want me to trust you, but I am not always sure I can. When I do, bear me up on the soft wind of your word, and let me soar to your glory.

Breezy

Theme: the child in you; surrender; holy play
Scripture: Lk 18:15-17
Feast: fourth Sunday after the Epiphany; All Saints
Sunday

("Warning: Cigarette smoking may be hazardous to your
health." Even non-smokers are familiar with these words.
They appear on billboards and cigarette packs. "Warning!" Sometimes stories ought to come with warnings at-
tached. The one that would accompany this story is:
"Warning! Reading this story with other than the mind
of the child in you may cause you to not understand its
message."

That does not mean that this is a child's story. It is not.
Rather, it is a story for the child that lies hidden in each
one of us — the child that struggles against an adult
world that has forgotten the words of Jesus: "Unless you
become like a little child, you cannot enter the Kingdom
of Heaven."

If you are willing to risk releasing that excited, playful,
happy child you are, you are invited to enter into the
story of "Breezy.")

Breezy was the offspring of two tropical depressions that formed southeast of Bermuda. They moved, almost side by side, toward land and then followed the east coast north to Cape Cod. From there they turned out to sea, and before they spent their fury, little Breezy spun off.

From the first, Breezy was filled with fun. He playfully skimmed over the surface of the wide ocean, gently lifting small waves and then letting them fall again. He liked looking for dolphins and riding on their backs as they swam close to the surface of the water. He found that if he spun around as fast as he could, he could cause water to rise and fall like a water fountain. Best of all he liked to catch birds in his gentle movements and carry them for miles and miles. Of course the birds liked being carried for long periods of time. They spread their wings and let the friendly little wind bear them to new and unknown places.

Well, Breezy moved as small winds do, somewhat erratically but in a general direction. In time he left the ocean's waters and blew over land. Much to his surprise, he had more fun over land than over water. Here he could carry children's kites high into the air; tumble dry leaves that had fallen from the trees; lift the down from thistles and watch as they floated gracefully like miniature parachutes. A little breeze could do so much. He even enjoyed making laundry move and dry as it hung behind people's cottages, or make flags flap as they hung on their standards.

As the weeks went by, little Breezy noticed a change coming over him. He was growing stronger. No longer was he a gentle friend to birds, but often blew them off course. No more did he play with children's kites or move laundry in a slow, easy wave. His winds were sharp and cold and unceasing. Although Breezy was not aware of it, he was also becoming destructive: pushing over trees whose roots had loosened their hold on the soft earth; upsetting tents erected to protect people from the elements; knocking down little toddlers just learning how to walk.

Minute by minute, hour by hour, day by day, he grew stronger. Soon his winds reached gale force. He blew dark, ominous clouds before him to announce that he was coming. People and animals ran for shelter from the force he brought with him.

Late one night, he released his growing power on a small country in the Middle East. A path of destruction was left in his wake. People ran in panic. Some were injured from objects Breezy blew over.

Soon he came upon a large lake. Breezy lifted the waves high into the air and sent them crashing into one another. The gale had become a hurricane that relentlessly unleashed his powers on the face of the lake. In the middle of the lake was a small boat tossing to and fro in the angry waters. The wind pushed at the side of the craft, nearly upending it and threatening to dump its frightened passengers into the boiling water.

Suddenly, a man in the back of the boat stood up, faced the storm, held up his hand, and said, "Peace. Be still."

Never had Breezy encountered such authority. Minute by minute the power of his wind diminished. The face of the lake calmed, and soon the boat was gently rolling and rocking in the lake's small swells. Breezy became what he had been before: a calm, gentle, playful breeze that liked to play with children's kites and ride on the backs of dolphins.

(But what, you may ask, does the child see as the meaning of this story?

Simply this: There rages in all of us the storms of life. Storms of anger, fear, mistrust, greed, loneliness, hopelessness, failure, insecurity, sin. But there is one, one whom we call Jesus, who stands, faces the storm, and says, "Peace. Be still" and calls out to the child in us, who in simple trust yields to his invitation and is led smiling, laughing, playing, dancing into the Kingdom of Heaven.)

Where is that child in me that once was filled with wonder and laughter? Did it grow up and forget how to be childlike? Did it become so serious that it forgot how to enjoy the simplicity of your grace? O Lord, take me in your arms and bless me and free that child that struggles against an adult world.

Hot Sand and A Gooseberry Bush

Theme: God's call; response
Scripture: Ex 3:1 - 4:17
Feast: third Sunday of Lent (C cycle)

Once upon at time in a land long ago and far away lived a very wealthy man who had many daughters. Both his riches and his daughters were a blessing to him. In those days a man's worth was measured by the size of his flock of sheep. Therefore, because he had many, many sheep, he was very rich. The only problem was that he didn't like sheep, so he depended on others to take care of them. That is where his daughters came in.

This man's daughters were not known for their beauty. In fact, neighbors considered themselves generous when they called them "homely." Regardless of their lack of beauty, the rich man managed to marry them off to men who were slow of wit and without work. With this strategy he not only provided husbands for his daughters, he also had built-in keepers for his growing flocks. It all made good business sense. His investments were being protected and at a very modest cost to himself. All it took were a few camel skins for their tents and extra broth in the stew when the family gathered at the end of the day to eat.

This story is about one of his sons-in-law, a rather moody young man who wandered in from the desert one day looking for a job. He was hired on the spot and in short time wed one of the rich man's daughters. However, he was not like the other men in the family. He sat off by himself for the most part and stared off into space, sometimes muttering something like "Where did I go wrong?" or "Why me?"

One day this young man was cresting a hill he had climbed in order to survey the land and see where he would next take the sheep. When he came over the rise, he saw a vision that he had never before perceived. He rubbed his eyes in disbelief. "It must be a mirage," he said to no-one in particular. "This sun is hot enough to cook anyone's brains." But he looked again and the vision remained.

"That's impossible," he said. "I remember my science teacher telling me that what I am seeing cannot happen. Yet, there it is."

Carefully he approached the strange sight before him. Before he got too close, he heard something strange. It sounded much like the static crackling of the atmosphere when a severe thunderstorm is nearing. He had seen the power of lightning and knew that he had better run for cover. But looking around, he found none.

Suddenly, a voice spoke to him,

"MOSES, TAKE OFF YOUR SHOES. YOU'RE STANDING ON HOLY GROUND."

And Moses said,

"Uh-huh! Is that you Jethro? Are you trying to scare me? You know I hate it out here with those dumb sheep, and the snakes and spiders and scorpions. Now, come out from behind that rock. And for goodness sake, dump some water on that bush you set on fire before you send the whole wilderness up in smoke."

Jethro did not come out from behind the rock. Instead, the air crackled and sparked and voice spoke again,

"MOSES, TAKE OFF YOUR SHOES. YOU'RE STANDING ON HOLY GROUND."

And Moses said,

"Say what? Do you know how hot that sand is? The sun's been beating down on it all morning and now some weirdo wants me to walk around barefoot like some circus performer walking on burning coals. Who are you, anyway? Is this some kind of fraternity initiation? If you think I'm going to take off my ... "

Moses' hair began to stand on end while dark clouds came together over where he stood. The air was so charged it seemed like the granddaddy of all lightning strikes was building up. The ground started to shake under his feet, and the voice said,

"MOSES, TAKE OFF YOUR ... "

"Okay, okay," Moses interrupted. "Look, I'm taking them off. See? Eee ... Ai ... Ouch! Jeez that sand's hot. There, are you satisfied? There's not enough water in all of Midian to cool my feet now ... Ouch ... Wow! What now?"

"MOSES, I HAVE HEARD THE CRYING OF MY CHILDREN. THEY ARE REALLY HURTING. I WANT YOU TO GO BACK TO EGYPT AND LEAD THEM TO FREEDOM."

Moses forgot about the burning sand and stopped his dancing. "Go back to Egypt?" he said, not believing what he heard. "Those turkeys are just waiting for me to go back. All I'll have to do is put one toe over the Mason-Dixon line and I'm crocodile meat."

At the mention of "toe," he realized that his feet were starting to blister, and he resumed his funny jig.

"No way Yahweh. You won't catch me within 100 kilometers of that place."

Again the dark clouds, cracking air, and trembling ground.

"MOSES ... "

What?! Moses shouted. "Leave me alone. I didn't call you. I was out here minding my own business; looking after those dumb sheep; making the best of a bad situation and you come along with this burning bush trick. How did you do that anyway?"

"NEVER MIND HOW I DID IT," the voice responded. "YOU WANT TRICKS, YOU'LL GET TRICKS. THE MAIN ISSUE IS, I WANT YOU TO GO BACK TO EGYPT."

"But why me?"

"YOU KNOW THE TERRITORY."

"Big deal! I also know that if you stick your hand into an adder's den you'll get bitten."

"MOSES, LISTEN TO ME. READ MY LIPS (HA! HA! HA!). I WANT YOU TO GO TO EGYPT AND FREE MY CHILDREN."

"Okay," Moses said, "suppose I do go back, how do you suggest I do what you want me to do?"

"TALK TO PHARAOH," the voice suggested.

"Now I know you've been standing in the sun too long, whoever you are. You think that old buzzard will even let me anywhere near his court, let alone talk to him? You seem to forget — there's still a price on my head. Besides, I've got you on this one. When it comes to talking and trying to convince people, I'm terrible. I can't put two words together that make sense."

"I KNOW. THAT'S WHY I'M GOING TO GIVE YOU SOME HELP. I AM STARTING TO GET THE FEELING THAT YOU ARE TRYING TO WEASEL OUT OF THIS. MAYBE I DIDN'T MAKE IT CLEAR. I'M NOT GIVING YOU A CHOICE."

"Sure, you're going to be a big success, sending a tongue-tied sheepherder to go one-on-one with the most powerful person alive. Something tells me you don't have all your camels in a line. I would need something that would get Pharaoh's attention."

"HM ... LET ME SEE," mused the voice. "WHAT CAN WE GIVE YOU THAT WILL MAKE WHAT'S-

HIS-NAME OVER THERE IN EGYPT SIT UP AND
TAKE NOTICE? YOU EXPRESSED SOME INTER-
EST IN MAGIC. OVER THERE, SEE THAT STICK?"
Moses nodded. "PICK IT UP."

Moses did as he was bid. He picked up the stick. It was
almost as tall as he was and nearly as thick as his wrist.

"NOW, THROW IT DOWN."

Moses shrugged his shoulders and threw the stick
down at his feet. Immediately the stick became a writhing
cobra.

"AIEEEEEEEEEAH!" Moses screamed and turned
white as a sheet. He forgot all about how hot the sand
was under his bare feet. In fact, he swore his feet became
two blocks of granite. Sweat poured out as the serpent
slithered around his feet.

"GEE I FORGOT. YOU ARE AFRAID OF SNAKES.
THE NEXT PART MAY BE A LITTLE DIFFICULT."

"W-w-w-what's that?" Moses stammered.

"YOU MUST PICK UP THE SNAKE."

Kerplop — Moses fainted dead away.

"MOSES. MOSES, GET UP. DO AS I SAY."

Fighting fear like he never had before, Moses reached
out with a trembling hand and grabbed the snake. *Voila!*
the snake became a stick again.

"OH GOOD, HERE COMES THE HELP I SAID I
WOULD GIVE YOU TO TALK TO PHARAOH. IT'S
YOUR BROTHER, AARON."

"O God, not Aaron," Moses moaned. "You're giving
me Aaron to be my spokesman? He's worse than I am. Do
you know he has never called me by my right name?
'Moze' ... He calls me 'Moze.'"

"Hey Moze, what's happening?" Aaron called out.

Moses cringed. "Nothing."

"'Nothing?'" Aaron questioned. "I come out here in
the middle of the wild and find you talking to a gooseber-
ry bush burning like a house on fire, and you say nothing
is happening?"

"It's a long story," Moses returned. "Come on, we have

a job to do." Then remembering one more thing, he turned back to the bush and said, "By the way, just in case someone should ask, who shall I say sent us? Who are you?"

The voice chuckled. "I THOUGHT YOU KNEW. YOU ALREADY USED MY NAME. I'M YAHWEH."

Moses shrugged his shoulders.

Aaron said, "I heard the question, bro; what was the answer?"

"Never mind," said Moses.

"Why?"

"You wouldn't understand."

"Why wouldn't I understand?"

"Because I don't understand," Moses said.

So the two brothers fell into step, side by side, and set their course toward Egypt, leaving the whole flock of Jethro's sheep stranded in the desert, which really ticked the old man off, but that's a different story. We leave the two brothers as we hear Aaron say to Moses,

"It was weird. There I was, sitting under the umbrella next to my kidney-shaped pool, sipping on a dry martini, when a voice comes out of the olive and says to me ... "

You speak to me, Father, in the shout of a sunset and the whisper of a rippling brook, Everywhere I meet you is holy ground. Open my ears to your voice as you speak, calling me to go to those in bondage. Let my battle cry be, "Let my people go."

Laura's New Dress

Theme: acceptance; absolution; God's love
Scripture: Rev 7:9,13-14
Feast: fourth Sunday of Lent (C cycle)

L aura had never felt clean most of her life. It wasn't that she didn't bathe. She did, often and fastidiously. But she never had a sense of having washed all of the dirt away. When Laura was a child, her parents were always after her to "clean up."

"Girls never get dirty," her mother used to say. "Go wash yourself." No matter how hard she tried, she was never able to get clean enough for her mother.

Her father always made it a point to remind her that to be a "good girl" and thus accepted by daddy, she had to lead a "clean life."

"Never do anything that will disgrace me," her father preached. As a result, Laura never believed that she could be good enough to earn her father's love, which came with such a price tag connected to it.

And church: "By thought, word, and deed." She had such deep guilt feelings. Little could she cope with the "unclean" thoughts that seemed to preoccupy her mind as a teen; or the few verbal flare-ups she experienced when she lost control of herself; or the actions she was certain were sinful, unclean, and ultimately damning. Usually while sitting in church, she would rub her hands together as though washing away the uncleanliness she felt, knowing all along that she would never find approval in the eyes of God.

This feeling of Laura's showed, though most people never were able to see or understand her plight. She could have been attractive, but really wasn't. "Poor Laura," people would say. "She's so homely."

Her straight hair looked as though it was cut while she wore a bowl on her head. Her pale skin was accentuated by the obvious absence of any make-up. Her clothes never were in style, and most hung like oversized bags, hiding any hint of a figure.

No wonder the people were so surprised when Laura got married. They had been convinced no-one would ever find her attractive enough to wed. Well, the truth of the matter is: the marriage was not out of love, but more for convenience. Pete had been a widower for about ten years and was lonely. That he married Laura for company was no secret, and Laura married Pete to try to escape her parents' constant reminders that she was never completely clean.

Unfortunately, even the marriage didn't work for Laura. Pete never accused her of being dirty, but Laura could feel it. She desired to be loving but could not give of herself freely. The few times she and Pete did sleep together were absolute nightmares because Laura remembered the words of her dad, and this was dirty.

When Pete died, Laura thought even less of herself. She blamed herself for not recognizing any signs that Pete wasn't well. Even though the doctor tried to reassure her that her husband had a chronic heart condition, Laura was sure that he died because she didn't do all she could, which made her feel all the more unclean. She even stopped going to church because she was certain that everyone there was pointing their fingers at her and blaming her for Pete's death. Surely she brought great disgrace upon her family.

Laura lived many years after Pete's death — more years than she really wanted to. And in all those years, she never ceased trying to rid herself of feeling dirty. But so deeply ingrained was this that physically, spiritually, emotionally, psychologically, she could never have a sense of being clean. How she admired all the people around her who smiled and all but glowed with cleanliness. She wished so much that she could believe the pastor's words when he spoke about being forgiven. Just once she would have liked to be attractive, both inwardly and outwardly. But it was never to be.

Laura died at the age of eighty-three, alone, sad, and still feeling unclean. When she was examined by the coroner, he commented at how soft and clean her skin was. After the paramedics had determined that she was dead, they looked around the small, comfortable living room in which she was found. It was absolutely spotless. Never had they encountered a home as free from dirt as Laura's. When some distant relatives came to claim the booty left to them by this strange woman, they found themselves completely taken by the neatness, orderliness, cleanliness, of Laura's home. When told about it, the neighbors said, "Too bad Laura never enjoyed herself. She always felt inferior for some reason or other. She was sure a hard one to get to know."

The story does not end there, because even though Laura never had a sense of being clean or acceptable or lovable or even forgivable, that didn't stop God from being God.

Much to her surprise, Laura was ushered into the presence of the Lord of Lords. There were no words of shame, no scoldings, no scowls of disapproval. Instead, a look of understanding was in his eyes. A thin smile traced his lips as a small tear glistened on his cheek. It was a look of both joy and sadness. He held out his hand to Laura and bid her come closer. As she did, he held out his other hand from which draped a dress.

No word was spoken, but Laura knew what had to be done. She took the dress and put it on. It was white as the purest snow. Laura literally shone radiantly. A beauty never before seen filled her with a sense of joy, completeness, and well-being. But most of all, while standing in the presence of the one who died and rose for her, for the first time in her existence — being loved, forgiven, accepted, and blessed — Laura was clean.

Am I good enough, Lord? You have washed my sins away, but am I really clean? So much about me makes me doubt it. What can you possibly see in me? I pray that though a sinner, you will still love me enough to forgive me and let me stand among your white-robed saints.

The Waiting Room

Theme: betrayal; sin
Scripture: Mk 14:17-21
Feast: Passion Sunday (B cycle, alternate); Maundy Thursday (B cycle)

The waiting room was hot, stuffy, and dingy. Ashtrays on stained, vinyl-covered end tables overflowed with crushed candy and gum wrappers, cigar and cigarette butts, and various other articles no-one would want to inventory. Magazines torn, tattered, and couponless littered the coffee table in front of a two-seater sofa. A dried-up fern drooped its lifeless stems over the side of its dusty pot and onto the top of a grungy, glass-covered plantstand.

In a chair next to the plantstand sat Leo, a short, pudgy man. He rocked the chair in which he sat on its two hind legs. A two-day growth of thick, bristly whiskers sprouted from his face. His trousers had long since lost their creases, and the cheap belt barely made its way around his rotund belly. His eyes were riveted to Millie, the young woman who sat directly opposite him on the left side of the sofa. She sat with her legs tucked under her, completely aware of the leering, hungry stares coming from the vulgar little man. She hid this awareness by pretending to be engrossed in the expert filing and buffing of her nails. Her artificial satin dress clung sensuously to the accentuated curves of her well-formed body. Next to her, on the sofa, sat Herb, a neatly dressed man, an executive type, who appeared to be the most "together" one of the group, except that he had the habit of chewing on his bottom lip in a worried manner. The fourth and last seat positioned next to the only door in the room was occupied by a man who sat forward, elbows on his knees and eyes downcast as he stared meaninglessly at his shoelaces.

Stifling a yawn, the female member of the group looked across the room and said, "Okay, Bozo, you looked and saw enough. You want to see more, you are going to have to pay for it."

Leo jumped out of his seat, stood with his hands on his hips and replied, "What the hell do you mean coming off like that? What do you expect the way you're dressed? You ain't making no attempt to hide what you've got."

"Well, what do you know," Millie taunted. "We've got a Harvard graduate among us."

"Will you two please stop," the nervous man demanded. "It's bad enough being crammed together in this stuffy room without having to put up with your bickering. I'm nervous as it is waiting for that door to open."

"Yeah," said Leo. "Doesn't that beat all? I've spent a lot of time waiting in line, but I never thought I'd have to wait to get into hell."

The girl's legs shot out from under her as she threw her nail file at Leo, who was standing in the middle of the room. "Shut up, you sleazeball!" she screamed. "We're not waiting to go to hell. We're simply sitting here until the time comes for our judgment."

"Well for me, they are one and the same," said Leo as he retrieved the file, which had missed him and landed at the feet of the man who sat hunched over. "My life doesn't leave much doubt as to what's going to happen to me. As far as I'm concerned, it's all over but the shouting."

"I do wish we would talk about something else," whined Herb. "All this talk about hell and judgment is making my ulcer kick up. If I knew it was going to be like this, I would have been more careful about how I lived my life."

"Oh, I don't know," returned Millie. "I think that is what is so hellish about all of this. I think we would have made the very same mistakes even though we know the results of them now. I don't think even I would have been any different."

An evil twinkle was in Leo's eyes when he said, "And I bet you could tell some pretty juicy stories. Why don't you make our waiting a bit more bearable by telling us some of your sordid memories?"

Millie started to cry. Herb clenched his fists and said, "If I was a violent man, I'd knock you senseless. You are disgusting. Do you always pick on people's weaknesses?"

"Yeah, I do. That was the only way to survive. Disarm the enemy before the enemy disarms you," replied Leo.

"But I'm not your enemy," Millie said through her tears. "I don't even know you, for heaven's sake. You didn't even give me a chance. If this is the way you always were, you must have been a very lonely man."

A brief interlude of silence filled the room. Millie dabbed at her tears with a tissue that she took from a small purse at her side. Leo sat down and started to rock on his chair. Herb rubbed where his stomach burned, and the silent one continued to study the floor in front of his feet.

Finally Herb spoke. "Maybe Leo has something. Since we have all this time, why don't we share the one thing that we lost as a result of the way we lived our lives? That way we don't have to dwell on the ugly details, but it might help us to get to know one another better."

"Tell us all about yourself," Leo said to Millie, "but don't listen to him. Don't leave out a single detail." He laughed and rubbed his hands together.

Fire danced in Millie's eyes. "Okay, I'll start. And to set your filthy mind at ease, yes, I was an escort."

"Oh, ho, ho," Leo teased, as he got up and danced around the room. "An 'escort' she was. For all the uninitiated in the room, that means she was a hooker."

Millie started to cry again. Her mascara ran into the blush applied to her cheeks.

"I was an *escort,*" she said between sobs. "Most people wondered why I did it. I guess it was mostly for the money — and the attention. I was always afraid of being alone and that no-one would pay attention to me. As an escort, I made a lot of money, lived well, and I was in demand because I was good. But now, I'm not sure it was worth it because even though I had all those things I thought were important, I lost my self-respect."

Her shoulders trembled as her sobbing became more violent. "Yes, I had what I thought I wanted: money, attention, clothes. But I came to that point in my life when I couldn't stand to look at my reflection in the mirror. What I saw was dirty and stained. That was when I decided to end it all. It was easy. A handful of pills and a glass of booze, and it was all over. What's the use of living if you can't live with yourself?"

For once Leo was quiet. The pain Millie shared affected everyone deeply.

"I wanted to be a success in business," Herb said to shatter the silence. "I started at the bottom. But all I needed was one glimpse of what it was like on the top and there was no stopping me.

"I soon learned that the only way to get around those who got in the way was to use whatever and whoever I could and discard them when I was finished. Soon it didn't matter if it was friend or foe. Everything became expendable if it prevented me from getting ahead — even my wife and children.

"That's where the breaking point came. I wanted to move ahead, and they wanted to stay where they were.

So, I unloaded them. Then one day, when I was just inches from the top, I realized I was losing. I had lost all meaningful relationships. And I found that not only did I have to keep looking forward to see how far I could go, but I also had to keep looking over my shoulder to see who might be gaining on me. The pressure drove me so hard that one night, while driving to an important business appointment, I was traveling too fast for the road conditions. All I could think about was making the deal; it meant a sure vice-president slot for me. But the car went out of control. The accident not only took my life, but also that of a family of five. I even went out at the expense of others."

Leo got up and started to pace. "You guys had it good! You had money, security, people who cared. Not me ... not Leo. I had to fight and grovel for everything I got. I was always being picked on. I was an unwanted child and my Ma always reminded me of the hardship I brought the family. My old man took off before I was born, and all I knew while I was growing up was the fact that we lived off the money Ma got from the 'friends' who visited her almost every night. So I built a wall around myself. If anyone stood in my way, I found their weakness and went after it. Right for the jugular."

Leo's face began to cloud over with a lifetime of emotion he thought he had controlled. In a soft voice, like that of a child that was alone and afraid, he continued. "I lost my sensitivity. I was so afraid of being hurt that I never considered that what I was doing to others was hurting them. My deepest pain was my unbearable loneliness. I died alone, in a cheap motel. I had too much to drink. I tripped and fell. My head hit the radiator and it was lights out."

Again silence reigned. They all felt a kind of emptiness. But much to their surprise, it did not feel uncomfortable. It was almost as if something they had carried for so long was removed, and they could stand straight again.

"What about you," Millie asked of the one who had said nothing so far. Not only had he been silent all that time, but he hadn't moved an inch.

Leo went over to him and said, "Come on, we all took our turn in the barrel. Now it's your turn."

Slowly, the quiet one lifted his head. His skin was as pale as death. He looked at each one of them through vacant eyes, as though the being that had once inhabited the body had abandoned it. They lacked color or sheen, and the pain of a thousand deaths was etched deeply into his frightened, tired face.

With a voice that was barely audible, he began. "I once had a friend, a dear friend. He meant the world to me. So many times he came to my rescue. He was always giving of himself for other people. One day when I was being criticized for the lifestyle I had adopted, he stood by my side and defended me. He even turned the argument of my attackers back on them to they ended up condemning themselves. He was so wise and compassionate, so understanding and forgiving, so full of goodness and rightness. We needed him to lead us, but he would have nothing to do with power. One day I decided that I would force him to take control. I had it all worked out so that he would have to act against those who were threatening us. But he still would have nothing to do with it. And instead of doing the right thing, I did the worst thing one friend can do to another."

At that the door opened, and the speaker stood and walked over to it. Slowly he turned and looked at Millie ... then Herb ... and finally Leo. "I betrayed him." As he turned to leave Herb called out. "But wait! What is it that you lost?" What little light that was left in his eyes was completely extinguished. They heard him say as he stepped over the threshold, "My Birth day. I lost my Birth day!"

Is it I? Can it be me? Do I betray you with my own sin? Must I keep on dying a thousand deaths? But no, there is forgiveness with you. I die my deaths only because I do not reach out and grasp your outstretched hand. Grant that I may never turn my back on you, but embrace you as my Lord and Savior.

The Day the Elephant Got Its Name

Theme: freedom with responsibility
Scripture: Gen 2:4-21a
Feast: first Sunday of Lent (A cycle)

Who does he think I am?" Adam muttered as he pushed his way through the underbrush of Eden. "'You're lonely, Adam. I'll make you some animals, Adam. Be the overseer of my creation, Adam. Give the animals names, Adam.' Big deal! That's easy for *him* to say. All *he* has to do is speak the word, and POOF! there it is. But I have to come up with all of the lousy names for those things he keeps creating. *He's* worse than a pair of rabbits.

"This is not an easy task. Oh, sure, the giraffe wasn't all that difficult; a giraffe looks like a giraffe. But the aardvark! Now that was a horse of a different color."

Adam made his way through some more thick brush, emerged into a clearing, and stopped dead in his tracks. His eyes opened so wide they appeared to be two round orbs fastened to either side of his nose.

"Oh my God!" he exclaimed.

"YES?" boomed a deep voice from behind him.

"Don't do that!" Adam shouted. "You keep sneaking up behind me like that and scaring me."

"WELL, WHAT WAS I TO DO? YOU CALLED ME."

"I didn't call you. I just said 'Oh my God.' It's an exclamation."

"THEN YOU'VE GOT TO BE MORE CAREFUL WITH YOUR EXCLAMATIONS. NOW, WHAT'S ALL THE FUSS?"

"It's that thing over there," Adam said, pointing in the direction of an animal standing in the center of the clearing. "I've never seen anything like it before in all my life."

"ADAM, YOU'VE NEVER SEEN ANYTHING LIKE ANY OF MY CREATIONS IN ALL YOUR LIFE."

"You know what I mean. That thing has left me speechless. It's so ... so ... "

"BIG?"

"Humongous is more like it. What is it?"

"ADAM, THAT'S YOUR DEPARTMENT, RE-MEMBER? I'M IN PRODUCTION. YOU'RE IN IDEN-TIFICATION AND LABELING."

"But look at it! Why did you make it so big?"

"I'M COMING TO THE END OF CREATION AND I HAVE A LOT OF MATERIAL LEFT OVER THAT I WANT TO USE UP."

"Well, I think you went too far. Where is an animal that big going to live?"

"ANYWHERE IT WANTS TO."

"The workmanship is not up to snuff. The skin is too loose. The ears are too large. And look at that tail. It's just too long. See how it drags on the ground. The poor beast doesn't know what to do with it. Now will you look at that! It actually lifted up that big head of cabbage with its tail and it's ... it's ... O God!"

"YES?"

"Now cut that out! I was just — oh never mind. Did you see what that dumb thing did with head of cabbage?

It picked it up with its tail and stuffed it right into its ... "

"ADAM. THE TAIL IS ON THE OTHER END."

"Oh, thank God."

"YOU'RE WELCOME."

"I guess I have to give it a name."

"RIGHT."

Adam looked at the large, sleepy-eyed beast for a long time. He walked around it, tried to span one of its legs with his arms. After a while Adam stepped back, stroked his chin with his hand, and thought hard about the name the animal was to have. Slowly, a smile formed on his face. "I think I have it."

"OKAY, TELL ME WHAT IT IS."

"How about, 'Heliphant.'"

"WHAT?"

"'Heliphant' — h-e-l-i-p-h-a-n-t," Adam spelled.

"WHY THAT, FOR MY SAKE?"

"Well, it is a hell of a fantastic animal. So I just combined the two words and came up with 'Heliphant.'"

"TELL YOU WHAT. DROP THE 'H' AND CHANGE THE 'I' TO AN 'E' AND I THINK YOU WILL BE ON TO SOMETHING."

"There you go again. You do it all the time. I suggest something and you change it. You said I have the right to make my own choices. Now, do I or don't I?"

"OF COURSE YOU DO, ADAM — EXCEPT WHEN I TELL YOU TO DO SOMETHING DIF- FERENTLY."

"That's not fair! Either I have it or I don't. I deserve it. I've been faithful. I've done this miserable job you gave me. This is one time I want it my way and not yours."

"ADAM, THAT ATTITUDE MAY GET YOU IN- TO TROUBLE ONE DAY."

"Nonsense. Now whose way will it be, yours or mine?"

"GUESS."

"Thanks a lot!"

"ADAM, I'VE NOTICED SOMETHING. I MADE
ALL THESE ANIMALS, BUT I SEE YOU ARE STILL
LONELY."

"Glad you noticed," Adam said.

"ADAM, LIE DOWN."

"Why?"

"I WANT YOU TO GO TO SLEEP."

"What if I don't?"

"YOU MUST."

"Free will, right?"

"RIGHT. NOW LIE DOWN!"

"Why?"

"I NEED A RIB."

*Abba, Father, you brought everything into being as a sign of
your gracious love and sense of humor. You laugh when I take
myself too seriously. You have given me a free will, but also
you have established limits and expectations. Forgive me when
I try to be the creator and am not satisfied being the creature.
Fill me with the good sense to laugh at myself when I forget
who I am.*

The Marriage of the Colors

Theme: harmony; unity; order in God's creation
Scripture: Gal 3:28; Gen 9:13a, 17; Mt 8:3
Feast: fifth Sunday after Pentecost (C cycle)

The life of a small child is filled with wonder and amazement and excitement. At least, Tommy's is. And this day was such a wonder-full day. It all began when he went outside, all bundled up against the crisp, autumn air. As soon as he stepped outside the door, he saw something he had never seen before. It looked as though smoke was coming out of his mouth. Every time he breathed out, a small wisp of vapor reached its fragile fingers upward and disappeared. Tommy stood on the steps for the longest time, breathing out and watching with fascination.

Then came the encounter with the woolly-bear caterpillar. Their meeting was quite by accident, and Tommy immediately considered this strange creature a newfound friend. He even let his furry buddy walk over the back of his hand, and that is when he discovered that caterpillars tickle when they walk. He wondered if they had as much fun walking over little boys' hands as little boys had letting them do it.

When the woolly-bear sauntered away, Tommy lay down on the grassy slope of a hill and watched as the clouds sped by. They looked like the sails of boats cruising by in a vast, light blue ocean. "I wonder," Tommy said to an ant that crawled by, "if Grandma is sailing in one of those boats. Mommy and Daddy said that's where Grandma went, and I bet she is looking down at me right now."

Well, it was one thing right after another, so much was stuffed into his busy day. Now it was nighttime, and Tommy sat at his pint-sized desk. He had in front of him a piece of heavy cardboard and three tubes of artist's paint that his Mother had given him. "Here," she said, "see what pretty colors and pictures you can make with this paint. But Tommy, make sure you keep the paint on the paper. Don't let any get on your desk or on the wall." Just to make sure, she had put some newspaper on the desktop.

He first picked up the tube of red paint, removed the top, and in the middle of the paper close to the top squeezed out a generous portion of the brilliant paint. Slowly it spread itself out an settled down into a neat pool. Inasmuch as it was oil-based paint, it did not spread too far.

For a couple of minutes, Tommy stared at the red paint. He saw by the way the light fell on the glob of paint that there was not just one color but many shades of red. He wondered what the yellow would look like. So he did the same with a good glob squeezed out on the lower left of the paper. It did the same as the red. In fact, it seemed as though some yellow reflected on the red and some red on the yellow.

Tommy completed his project by putting some blue paint on the lower right of the paper. Then he settled down to watch and see what new adventures the paint had for him. He spread his arms on the top of the desk, interlaced his fingers, and rested his chin on the top of one of his hands. And he stared, and stared, and stared ...

Naturally, nothing happened. That is, nothing happened until the pool of red paint began to quiver. All of a sudden, a small column of paint stood straight up and said, "Boy, am I glad to get out of that tube."

To Tommy's amazement, the yellow did the same thing. Only, instead of a column, it raised and twisted so that it represented a yellow, soft ice cream cone. "You can say that again," Yellow said. "It was getting cramped in my tube."

Not to be left out, Blue also responded. Only when it rose up, it slowly began to bend over. "Oh, I don't know," Blue said sadly. "It's not any better out here. That air makes me stiff. If I stay out here, I won't be able to move at all."

Oh, how Tommy wanted to talk to the paint too. But like all other children, Tommy knew that when people talk, the magic spell is broken. He didn't want it to stop, so he kept as quiet as a mouse and tried not to move at all.

"Blue," Red said, "why is it that you are always so negative and depressing?"

"I don't know," Blue answered. "I guess it is just my nature. Blue is always said to be sad, and cold. People say they are 'blue' when they don't feel very happy. I don't know why. They don't look at all like me."

"Well at least you have a strong point. How would you like to be yellow?" said Yellow. "I represent cowardliness and weakness. People who are afraid are said to be 'yellow.'"

"Yeah," said Red. "Sometimes I get tired of being just me. I wonder what I would be like if I were different."

"Hey!" shouted Blue. "That gives me an idea. Why don't we become something different than we are?"

"That doesn't sound like a very safe idea," quivered Yellow. "We've never done anything like that before."

"Oh, come on, Yellow," said Blue. "Don't be so ... so ... "

"Yellow!" helped Red. "Yeah, come on, let's see what happens."

Blue thought a bit and then said, "I know, we will have marriages. We will all give part of ourselves to another color and then see what happens."

"I'm going to go first," Red informed the others, "and I want to be wed to a part of Yellow. Maybe between my temper and your fear, something good will happen. Come on, Yellow, loosen up. Give me a part of yourself."

Red separated so that a portion of itself moved toward Yellow. All the way, it coaxed Yellow until finally a part of Yellow did the same. The two colors met and then began to twirl around and around, faster and faster until you could not distinguish Red from Yellow. When the spinning stopped, there lay a brilliant, beautiful pool of orange paint. Tommy's eyes opened wide. He had never seen that magic before.

"Let's see," said Orange. "What is colored orange?"

Orange moved and on the paper began to draw a pumpkin. That was followed by a beautiful, autumn leaf, just like Tommy had seen outside earlier in the day. Next appeared a delicious-looking carrot. Tommy could hardly keep himself from clapping his hands. How he loved to eat carrots, especially when they went CRUNCH. Sometimes they would make so much noise that his parents would tell him to eat more quietly. Tommy wished that his mother and father could find out how much fun it was to eat noisy foods noisily.

Just when Orange was ready to make another picture, Blue decided that it would be nice to be wed to a color too. Blue said, "Red, I wonder what would happen if there was a marriage between you and me?"

"Well," replied Red, "let's find out."

So Red and Blue came together, twirled around and around, and when it stopped, it was the most beautiful purple Tommy had ever seen.

Immediately Purple set to work. "Plums are purple; Purple Martins are purple; kings' robes are purple; shadows are purple." Each time something was mentioned, it appeared. Tommy watched. The plum made his mouth water; the bird looked so real that it seemed to fluff its feathers; the robe made him think of King Arthur; and the shadow looked just like the one that always followed him around.

"There's only one more move to make," Yellow said. "Blue, you and I need to be married."

"What a combination that will make," replied Blue. "With your fear and my depression, who knows what will happen."

So they wed, and yes, the result was green. Not sick green or putrid green, but a nice, friendly green. Green made green grass and a green katydid and a green dragon (the friendly kind, of course).

Tommy couldn't keep quiet anymore. He was so excited that he laughed and clapped his hands at once.

That scared all of the colors. They began to run about and finally came together in a frenzy of activity. What was left behind was a beautiful rainbow that came from the colors scurrying about, and a deep, rich brown where they met. The brown looked like the ground that smelled so good when Daddy dug in his garden.

Then Tommy heard his name being called. "Tommy ... Tommy ... Tommy ... " He felt a hand on his shoulder, gently shaking him. Tommy opened his eyes; he had fallen asleep.

His mother began to laugh. "Look at your hands, Tommy."

He looked at his hand and saw that his fingertips were covered with colors. This one was blue; the next yellow; then red and orange and purple and green on his other hand. The palm of one hand was all brown.

"Oh! Look, Tommy," his mother said, "what a beautiful picture you painted."

In front of the sleeping boy was a picture. Green grass grew out of rich, brown soil. A tree with orange leaves stood off to the side, and on a branch of the tree sat a tiny bird. A king was walking through his garden, looking at the pumpkins and carrots while eating a plump, juicy plum. Behind the king followed the shadow like an obedient subject. On top of the pumpkin, a katydid sat ready to sing her song for the queen, and off in the distance the gentle dragon waited for the children of the realm to come and play.

And over the whole picture arched the most beautiful rainbow ever drawn by a child. It was truly a beautiful picture. And Tommy knew that it was the marriage of the colors that made it all possible.

Lord Jesus, who as a boy played with the imagination of a child, and who held up childlikeness as an example of those who shall live eternity with you, keep alive this amazing wonder so that clouds and caterpillars, colors and pinecones will reveal your creative genius and call us out to play.

The Ssserpent's Sssad Sssaga

Theme: temptation; loss of innocence
Scripture: Job 1:6-7; Gen 3,4
Feast: third Sunday after Pentecost (B cycle)

T hisss is certainly a ssserious sssituation," mused the serpent as he slithered along the sunbaked soil. "In fact, the whole sssituation ssstinks!" His slinky body sinuously slid sideways down a sandy slope. "Sssee what I mean?" the serpent sadly stated. "Sssuch embarrassment I have never had to endure before. I used to be sssure of foot. Now I don't even have a leg to ssstand on. How humiliating it is to have to crawl around on one's ssstomach. The worst part is getting sssand in my eyes. I have to learn to hold my head up higher. But when I do, I get such a pain in my back."

Tears came to his eyes as he thought about how things used to be. "I used to be able to sssit in the treetops and sssurvey the whole kingdom just as it was. I was a right good sort of guy. Some called me sssubtle. Others sssaid I was crafty or cunning. That may be true. But if I have to sssay ssso myself, I was a ssstunning sssight.

"But I never was one to do things right. I had to be in

that particular tree on that particular day, didn't I? I just couldn't help myself. I sssaw an opportunity and grabbed at it. That woman came along and before you know it, we were talking about what is forbidden and what is not. Ssso what if you can tell the difference between what is good and what is evil. Who wants to be innocent anyway? And if it looks good, why not taste it?"

The serpent was so engrossed in his thoughts that he didn't see the sharp stone sticking out of the ground. Before you could flick your tongue, he ran right over the sharp edge of the stone. "Ouch!" he hissed. "That sssmarts. Sssee what I mean? No self-respecting ssserpent should have to go around in as demeaning manner as this!

"Then there was that fateful day when He found out what happened. Oh yesss, I finally did convince the woman to sssnack on that succulent fruit. Then she talked her mate into tasting it. As sssoon as they both took a bite, sssomething happened. They took one look at each other, and they realized that neither of them had any clothes on. Well, you should have ssseen them. They ssstood there trying to cover themselves with their hands. There was no way they were going to hide what they had.

"Ssso the man, thinking himself to be resourceful, ran into the forest and came back with sssuper large leaves out of which they made clothing. To watch it all almost made the whole incident worthwhile.

"Well, they couldn't keep what they did a sssecret very long. He was bound to find out sssomehow. And when He did, all hell (if you will pardon the expression) broke loose. Boy was He mad! He pointed his finger at the man and sssaid, 'Man, what have you done?' It sounded like thunder.

"But really, don't you think that was a bit much? He knew what happened. Just one look at the man was enough. Guilt was written all over his face. And then guess what he did. He turned toward the woman and sssaid, 'She made me do it!'"

The serpent started to snicker just thinking about the scene. "Well," he continued, "she ssstarted to sssputter and sssspit, not knowing what to say. And that'sss when I got dragged into thisss whole messs. She put all the blame on me. When He heard that, His face got all red. I thought He was going to blow a gasket. I ssswear I ssssaw sssmoke come out of His ears. And that'sss when he ssstarted to dish out all of the punishments. Before I knew it, I was crawling around on my belly.

"Then He turned to me and sssaid, 'I will put an enmity between you and the woman, and between your off-spring and hers. He will crush your head and you will strike his heel.' The trouble is He didn't sssay anything about the woman and her damned club. I met her today as she was on her way to the well, and do you know what she did? First, she ssscreamed bloody murder, and then she came after me with this board. I think she actually wanted to pound me into the ground. She called her mate, but he took one look at me and fainted dead away. Oh well, sssuch is the life of a sssimple ssserpent.

"Now that I'm out of the garden, too, I guesss I will have to find sssomething else to do. Maybe I will start with those two young men over there. They ssseem to be in a pretty ssserious argument. Let's sssee if I can find out what it is all about. Yesss, I understand. One brother is angry because his sssacrifice was not acceptable when his brother's was."

Loving God, whose heart breaks at our rebellion and who willingly gave up his own son, preserve us from the crafty wiles of Satan and prepare us to share your glory in eternity.

Reverend Billy's Church

Theme: honesty; self-examination
Scripture: Ps 139:24
Feast: third Sunday of Easter (B cycle)

("Good morning," the pastor says as he greets his parishioners at the church door, "how are you today?"

"Oh, fine, pastor," the voice says while the eyes betray the pain or the anxiety or fear that plagues the lives of those to whom he tries to bring the message of the Good News.

Masks. People, clergy, and lay wear masks trying to hide the true self; afraid to betray any kind of human weakness. And all along, the human spirit calls out for some sign of hope.

Sometimes these masks slip, or through loving care is allowed to be removed. And what is found behind the mask is the child whom Christ calls out of us. It is the child that needs the constant affirmation of his or her parents' love; the child that longs for the words of forgiveness over and over again.

Do we ever tire of the repetition of the Gospel? I believe not. Rather, the only thing that remains constant is our need to confess that we have indeed sinned in thought, word, and deed, and though deserving God's condemnation, we receive God's grace as a free gift that keeps on coming like that of an ever-flowing, country stream.

What secrets are hidden behind the masks of those who come into the presence of the Lord? Where is the line of distinction between what is real and what is false? When is our outward countenance genuine and when is it a facade?

Listen to the words of the Psalmist: Search me, O God, and know my heart; Try me, and know my anxieties; And see if there is any wicked way in me, and lead me in the way everlasting" [Ps 139:24]).

Reverend Billy Bob Hardgrave stood in front of the massive doors that opened into the sanctuary of his church. He could always be found there just before he would make his grand entrance to begin the service. The muffled sounds of the clicking castanets keeping time to the upbeat organ music filtered through to Reverend Billy. The organist liked to use that setting on the brand new, option-laden, electronic organ, but Reverend Billy preferred the Big Band sound. Tears could be seen welling in his eyes when he sang "I'm Safe In His Hands," accompanied with trombone and trumpet background. "Yes sir," he would say to himself, "these new organs are electronic marvels."

These moments before the start of the service were Billy Bob's meditation time. Usually he would meditate on how fortunate he was to have this location for his church. The major highway that passed in front surely was one reason he always "played" to a full house. Other times, he would beam over the filled-to-capacity parking lot that adjoined his First Church of the Once-And-For-All Decision.

Today, however, his meditation reflected on that fateful day six years ago when he received his call into the ministry. It was one of those days (there were so many of them) when he got himself into a situation he could not escape. He had inherited the garage from his father, but he was never a very good mechanic. Often he would take something apart and not be able to get it together again. Frustrated with an insurmountable problem, Billy Bob locked himself in his office and began to leaf through his pile of outdated magazines.

Almost as if by divine intervention, the ad jumped out at him: UNHAPPY WITH LIFE? ENROLL IN OUR SCHOOL. He read on with rapt attention. "Has life got a stranglehold on you? Would you like more than what you're getting? For just $25, you can enter our correspondence school and earn your degree!"

"Wow!" Billy thought to himself, "This might be my answer."

But, what kind of degree would he get? The ad listed all of the degrees that could be bought: electronics, book binding, appliance repair, lawn ornaments, pipe fitting, theology, landscaping, computer technology ... *Theology!*

"That's it! The hand of the Lord is upon me!" he shouted out loud. "I am today's Isaiah. Here I am Lord. Send me!"

He closed down the garage that day. The owner of the car he was working on had to have it towed to another garage. Never again did he look at the motor of a car. He was now doing the Lord's work. He had made a once-and-for-all decision.

Before the day was over, Billy Bob mailed his check to The School of Diplomas for Every Occasion. Within a week he had his first lesson, and before three days passed, the completed booklet was in the return mail.

In no time at all he completed his course, and with the very last session, he included his $50 payment for graduation and diploma. Billy Bob could hardly wait to get his certificate and begin his ministry.

As soon as he finished his lessons, he put down a payment on a parcel of land that adjoined the Interstate. Then he found a contractor who was willing to put up the building that Billy Bob designed. Every day, he visited the site and personally oversaw the construction. In the evenings, he started making visits and phone calls and soon had the interest of a group of people to start a congregation when the building was completed. His enthusiasm was so contagious that, after showing his plans and talking about his ministry, he had enough money to pay for the church and the paving of the parking lot. He seemed to be a natural.

Finally the diploma came and the building was finished. The day was filled with excitement as they pulled the drape from the signboard in the front of the church and opened the doors for the first time. The congregation broke into spontaneous applause when they saw the name of the church emblazoned in neon lights on the sign that was made in the shape of an ascending dove. When asked if he didn't have it wrong — shouldn't the dove be descending? — he would answer, "No siree. Once the Eeeternal Speerit has lit upon you, it can go on home because it has done its work."

Satisfied, Reverend Billy turned to enter the church to make his dramatic entrance. He looked one last time at his church. It stood like a castle casting its shadow on the world around it. High towers rose from the front two corners of the building. From the top of the left tower jutted a stainless steel cross, and out of the right tower rose a flagpole from which flew a banner with an ascending dove.

The front of the building was made of imitation stone. It didn't seem to bother anybody that the sides and back of the building were unpainted and unadorned concrete block. To the trained eye, the church represented the facade of a Hollywood set castle. But to the members of the Church of the Once-And-For-All Decision, the front of the church was what they were proud of. This was their fortress, even if it was only the front.

However, the church was not the only one with the false front. Reverend Billy Bob always feared that which hounded his heels through his whole life: failure. The "Halleluias" and "Praise the Lords" and "Preach to us, Billys" buoyed him against his fear of failure. Standing in the pulpit with his arms uplifted, he broke into his song, "I'm Safe In His Hands."

The organist, picking up the cue, quickly switched on the Big Band sound while his fingers automatically punched out the familiar tune. His thoughts, however, were on the bottle of whiskey that waited for him at his small, empty apartment.

Susan Wellington beamed up at Reverend Billy Bob, looking pure and innocent, but her heart raced at the thought of the rendezvous planned with the head usher's son. That he was married and had two children mattered little to her. After all, if it was kept a secret, what harm could come of it?

Charlie Evans, president of the First Local Bank, the most generous giver in the congregation, rehearsed the speech he would use when he would inform the Widow Perkins that she would lose her house due to non-payment of bills. It was not all that unpleasant to him; it made widows very vulnerable.

All around the church, rapture-filled eyes were riveted on the figure in the pulpit. They were all there because the Holy Spirit "lit" upon them, and they were saved by their once-and-for-all-decision. But inside each one of them gnawed the dis-ease of the human condition. The masks they wore hid the pain and suffering that tore at their lives. The words they heard, the songs they sang, the ecstasy they felt was as false as the front of The First Church of the Once-And-For-All Decision.

It is so easy to pretend to be what I am not. It is also safer not to let others see me as I really am. I wear my mask; I hide my true self, but you know me and search me. I can hide nothing from your eyes. Make me what you would have me be and fill me with your truth.

Ol' Sam's Secret

Theme: aloneness; loneliness; presence of Christ
Scripture: Mt 28:20
Feast: Holy Trinity (A cycle)

The villagers who lived around The Point didn't think Ol' Sam would stay on after Kate died. They were as close as any couple they knew. No-one could remember either one of them saying anything like "I love you" in public, but then, they didn't have to. You could see it in their eyes, the way they looked at each other, and how Kate would put her hand on her husband's when he stood behind her with his hands on her shoulders.

Kate died peacefully in her sleep. Ol' Sam was so thankful that she didn't have to suffer in any way. But his pain was deep. No-one saw him for many days following the funeral. People were afraid that he too had given up and died. Finally, some of his closest friends elected a representative to go and see if he was okay. Ned, the postmaster from North Bay, drew the short straw. He was afraid of what he was going to find. As he came close to The Point, he saw Ol' Sam bent over in his small garden, hoeing out the weeds with such vigor that he appeared to be battling more than the weeds that threatened to take over.

Well, Ol' Sam had not only recovered from his grief, but much to everyone's surprise, he even decided to stay on at The Point. Being the keeper of a lighthouse was lonely enough when one had a mate, and now many wondered how he was going to stand it being alone.

They were glad, however, that he did decide to stay because he was the most faithful keeper of the light known along the whole eastern coast. Night after night, without fail, his beacon sent out its signal warning of danger and his foghorn blew at the slightest sign of a mist gathering. Ol' Sam was a dedicated lightkeeper and a friend of all the fishermen in the villages.

Many times he put his life on the line for someone else. No-one would ever forget the night a strong gale blew. The sea was angry and pounded its thunderous fist against the rocks. The beacon seemed extra bright that night and the foghorn sounded louder than ever before.

Ol' Sam kept a constant vigil that night. It was a good thing he did, too. At first he wasn't sure he was seeing right. It looked like a small boat was in trouble and was being pushed closer and closer to the murderous rocks. He ran for his binoculars and saw what he had hoped was not there. A cabin cruiser was in distress, and he could make out at least two people on her deck. He called quickly to Kate and told her to raise the Coast Guard on the radio. He slipped into his nor'easter and ran to the dock where his motor launch was moored.

That launch was Sam's pride and joy. She might have been ancient, but she was powerful and dependable. He was his own mechanic, so he knew he could trust his own life with her.

After he cast off the lines, Ol' Sam fought the vicious tide. The sea seemed hell-bent on claiming life that night. But he made it safely to the crippled boat and rescued a young couple and sixteen-month-old baby. As Sam maneuvered the launch back to the dock, they watched their boat splinter to pieces as the waves dashed it without mercy against the rocks.

Ol' Sam and Kate took the couple and their baby into the warm, cozy lighthouse apartment. They gave them dry clothes to wear and blankets to drape over their shoulders. Kate fussed about in the kitchen as she brewed some hot tea. And as she was known to do, she also muttered to herself. "Dam' fool thing to be out on that water on a night like this — and with a small child to boot. Not an ounce of sense in either of their heads. Who in their right minds would want to sail a boat anyway — nothing but a dam' nuisance ... " She muttered on and on without showing a single hint of genuine anger.

Sam chuckled and told them to give her no mind. "If she wouldn't be fussin' over you, she'd be chewin' at me. Gives me a rest having her take on after someone else," he said, his eyes twinkling as he sat back and puffed on his pipe.

Yes, that's the way Ol' Sam and Kate were. After Sam faced his loss head-on, that's how he continued to be. The light from the lighthouse burned as bright and the foghorn sounded as clear as ever. He continued to put his life on the line, tinkered with his launch, and walked the high balcony as he waited for the fishing boats to return before the sun set. He knew all of the skippers by name and would wave a greeting as they went out and came back.

Ol' Sam was a bit of a puzzle to the villagers. He had a source of strength that enabled him to keep going unlike anyone else they knew. He lived as though he knew a secret, and that secret was the source of his strength. They knew he missed Kate. But they felt that Ol' Sam lived on as though she was still with him. He didn't withdraw like they thought he would. He continued to go to church, was the first one at the church socials, still taught young boys how to tie all of the important knots, carved small boats, and even built a few in glass bottles.

Ol' Sam was the talk of the villagers. How could he be so peaceful? How did he remain so composed? How could he stand being alone in that lighthouse? How could he cope with the death of his beloved Kate?

One night, all of these questions were answered. Little did Cap'n Henry realize that as he piloted his fishing boat through the opening in the quay that he was the one who would make the discovery.

At first he didn't know what was wrong, but he sensed something amiss. He stood on the bridge of his boat, his face to the wind, squinting his eyes. He tried to put his finger on what it was that made him uneasy. He looked toward the lighthouse and then realized what it was. The light was not burning. "Ol' Sam would have had that light burning by now," he said to himself. As a cold shiver ran up and down his spine, he knew something was wrong.

Cap'n Henry changed course and headed for the dock where the ancient launch was tied up. He quickly walked up the narrow path that led to the door of the lighthouse. He knocked and waited. No response. He didn't even hear a stirring inside.

Cap'n Henry tried the doorknob. It was unlocked. He stepped inside and called, "Sam. Sam ... " but there was no answer. The apartment was clean and neat, but there was no sign of his dear friend.

Slowly he climbed the circular staircase that led to the second level where Ol' Sam kept all of his nautical tools. He didn't have to climb all the way up before he saw the keeper of the light. He was seated at the chart table. The top was littered with maps. Ol' Sam did not stir. His head was laying down on the table top, cradled in the bend of his arms as though he were asleep. In front of him was an open book, and his right hand was resting on one of its pages. Cap'n Henry realized, as he drew closer, that the book was Sam's old Bible, which he carried with him every Sunday when he went to church. Sam's finger pointed to a verse in the Bible.

Cap'n Henry bent over Sam's lifeless body and read the verse. Then he knew Sam's secret. He knew where he got the strength and the faith to keep going in spite of great loss. Cap'n Henry knew how Sam could keep living as though Kate was still as his side; how he could sing hymns of joy and gladness in church with such off-key gusto; how even in death Ol' Sam could be at peace. Cap'n Henry read again, "Lo I am with you always ... "

Lord, help me to know that I am never alone. You promised to be with those you love and to never abandon them. Open my mind and heart to your presence and enable me to erase the loneliness in the lives of others by being your presence to them.

The First Gift

Theme: Incarnation; Christmas; birthplace for Christ
Scripture: Lk 2:4-7
Feast: Christmas Eve or Christmas Day

(It is true that the Christmas season can have its seamier side. One cannot be confronted by the commercialism and consumerism, the lists of wants, or the contrasting display of wealth in the presence of squalor without realizing that the celebration of this holy time can certainly be misguided and misdirected.

Having said that, one must also realize that Christmas is a very special time of the year that can bring out the best in us. It is ...

A time for family meetings
  and wishing of Merry Christmas greetings
A time for being jolly
  and hanging of mistletoe and holly
A time for sweet smells of freshly baked Christmas cakes
  and "Away in the Manger" where "no crying he makes."
A time for Silent Night, Holy Night
  and a world gone wrong again put right.
A time for familiar carol singing
  and the excitement of love-from-the-heart gift
    bringing.

Christmas is also a time for familiar storytelling. In the telling of the story, the faith is kept alive, hope is re-kindled, and we are once again brought into the presence of the divine mystery, who loves this world and its people so much that he gives his only begotten son.

So in the tradition of a time long ago and far away, gather and listen as the teller of stories once again weaves his verbal tapestry in the pattern of faith. Listen, my children, as I tell you the story of The First Gift.

Gift-giving has always been a part of the celebration of the birth of Jesus. The Gospel writer Matthew makes much out of the visit of three men of wisdom from the East who brought their gifts of gold, frankincense, and myrrh. It is not too hard to imagine the shepherd who heard the heavenly choir sing bringing the gift of a lamb to the Christ child. Many stories have been written and told about gifts from unemployed jugglers to little drum-mer boys. Tonight I want to tell you the story about the very first gift.)

Samuel drew his cloak closer to his body as he quick-ly walked through the near-deserted streets of Beth-lehem. His little inn was filled to capacity with hungry travelers — thirsty too! That is why he tugged impatiently at the reins of his old, tired, wineskin-laden donkey. "By Jehovah," he swore under his breath, "why did I have to run out of wine on the coldest night of the year?"

Again, he yanked impatiently on the reins. "Come on, you lazy beast," he shouted with mock anger. "If you go any slower, the wine will turn to vinegar."

In just a few minutes he saw the warm glow of the lights from his inn. His old bones yearned for the heat of the main room where a fire glowed in the hearth and people shared tales. With a sigh of relief, he tied his beast to the post and lifted one of the bulging skins of wine to his shoulder.

A round of applause from his guests greeted him as he entered the crowded room. He caught sight of his wife,

Hannah, who was serving a table on the other side of the room. She looked tired, and when their eyes met she told him that she was glad he had returned. Samuel noticed that his wife looked exceptionally worried or bothered.

As soon as she set the steaming plate of mutton on the table in front of the hungry pilgrims, she made her way toward her husband, wiping her hands on her soiled apron. "Samuel," she said, "I am so relieved you are back. Please go outside, in the courtyard. See if you can help them, poor souls."

Samuel knew that meant trouble. Hannah was always a soft touch for people with a sad story. But he had long since learned that if he wanted peace, he would do as his wife said.

When he stepped into the courtyard, he was met by a young man standing next to his beast of burden, upon which sat a young girl, hardly out of her teens. When the young man saw Samuel, he whispered something to the girl and approached him. "Kind sir," the young man said, "please, my wife and I need a place to stay. We have come all the way from Galilee so that I can register for the census, and we are very tired."

"Oh Hannah," Samuel said to himself, "why do you always do this to me?" To the young man he said, "But I have no room. There isn't a spare inch. I have travelers sleeping on tables at night. I would like to help you, but I cannot. You will probably have to go to Bethany. You may find some room there."

The traveler looked disappointed but said, "I understand. It's just that ... well ... you see ... my wife is with child and her time is soon. Her pains have already begun, and we cannot go much farther."

Samuel was filled with a deep sorrow. He wanted to help, but he could not. Where could he possibly put them? And where, pray tell, could this poor woman have her child in privacy?

At that moment the young girl raised her head and looked at him. Her innocent beauty took his breath

away. It seemed as though her face reflected the glow
from the windows of the inn. Samuel's plight made his
heart ache all the more; there was no way he could help
them.

But then he remembered. "Young man — " Samuel
began.

"Joseph. Please call me Joseph," he interrupted. "And
this is Mary, my wife."

"Joseph, it is not much, but you might find staying in
the stable over there ... " Samuel pointed to the other side
of the courtyard ... "to be comfortable enough. It is
warm, well protected from the wind. My boy just cleaned
it out this afternoon. You can have that. And I will have
my wife bring you and Mary a nice warm meal."

With a voice as soft as the fluttering wings of a dove,
Mary spoke. "Thank you, Samuel. You are most kind.
We will stay in the stable. For Joseph and me, it will be as
glorious as Herod's palace."

Joseph smiled, shook Samuel's hand, and picked up
the donkey's reins. Slowly he led the animal to the stable,
carefully lifted his wife off of the beast's back, and helped
her into the waiting refuge from the cold.

Samuel ran back into the inn. "Hannah," he called
out, "hurry up, I think you will be needed in the stable."

Even while he was calling out his concern, his wife appeared, arms filled with birthing clothes and binding
cloth. She was followed by their servant girl, who carried
a tray of hot, steaming food. Hannah had known all
along that Samuel would help. She also knew that he
needed to think that he actually made the decision to
help. Samuel wondered at his wife's amazing intuition.

Well, it was a wonder-full night. The child was born, a
healthy and strong baby boy. The birth cries of the baby
sent up a whoop of happiness in the dining room.
Samuel was so relieved, he ordered the serving boy to give
each guest a free draught of wine.

But that is not all that happened that night. Shepherds
in the field came telling of a vision of angels and the sing-

ing of an anthem. People of all stations in life visited the stable to see this newborn baby, who was born under such strange and amazing signs.

Time passed and the day came when Joseph and Mary and baby Jesus had to leave Bethlehem. This was shortly after the visit of the three astrologers from the East, who brought expensive gifts for the child.

Samuel and Hannah hated to see them go. They had secretly adopted them during their stay. Hannah loved sitting next to Mary and holding the infant in her arms, remembering years long gone by when she held her own Josh and nursed him at her breast.

But the time had come. Joseph seemed driven by some urgency to leave. Samuel went out to the stable to see if he could help the new family prepare for the journey. He carried a sack of food that would nourish them on their way.

After all was ready, Samuel looked on this special child for the last time. He smiled as he watched the baby Jesus try to maneuver his uncoordinated fist to his mouth and laughed at the little squeak he let out in protest when his fist hit his eye instead.

"Joseph," Samuel said, "I am sorry to see you go. I am sorrier that I did not give you a more suitable gift. The shepherds brought you a lamb, the Magi, the treasures of the East, but I have nothing to give."

"But my friend," Joseph protested, "you have given us the best gift of all. You gave the first gift."

"Yes, Samuel," Mary added. "When we had no place to stay, you made room for us here. You fed us, gave us the birthing clothes, and let us stay here until we were strong enough to move on. You gave the gift of a place for Jesus to be born."

"Good-bye, Samuel," Joseph said. "And thank you."

Joseph, Mary, the baby, and the donkey slowly began to walk away from the inn. As they passed the door to the inn, they looked up and saw Hannah fighting back her tears. Mary and Joseph smiled warmly at her, and it seemed as though the baby Jesus actually waved.

No greater gift can you give this night to the Christ child than a place in your own heart and life for him to be born.

What can I give you, Lord? Riches are nothing in your sight. You have more power. Success is of no importance. It must be true then that all I can give you is a place to be born within me. Grant me grace to open the door of my heart, that you may dwell in me and I in you.

The Bouquet

Theme: Christ to others
Scripture: Mt 1:22-23
Feast: fourth Sunday in Advent (A cycle)

Not long after Anna became homebound, her neighbors realized that every Wednesday afternoon, Leonard, her son, and his wife Jeanine came to visit. They admired him for his loyalty because it was a bit of a hardship for him. Leonard was not poor, but he did not have much to spare. He did not own a car, so he and his wife had to walk from the other side of town. It is safe to say that they lived a very simple and frugal life. They had just enough to get by on. And for Leonard and Jeanine, that was enough.

No, they didn't miss a Wednesday, no matter what the weather, fair or foul, Wednesday after Wednesday, week after week, Anna received her visit from her son and daughter-in-law. Anna's neighbors admired Jeanine just as much. Except for a few weeks after the twins were born, she could be seen trudging along at her husband's side. Then even when the twins came, on many cold, winter days, Leonard and Jeanine could be seen each carrying a tiny bundle of blankets in which was one of the children.

Anna loved to see the twins, and they enjoyed their weekly visit with Grandma. "My, how big they are getting," she said every time they came. Leonard and Jeanine would smile at each other, and Jason and Joan would feel a sense of pride. It was exciting to grow up and Grandma made them feel good.

Grandma's house was filled with many treasures to discover. And she did not mind when they found something new and asked if they could play with it. Most of all, they liked to play her wind-up Victrola. They would turn the crank, put a record on the turntable, place the needle in the first groove, and sit and listen. Jason like to open and close the little doors in the front that made it sound like the singer was in a closed room.

So it was that Leonard, Jeanine, Jason, and Joan spent their Wednesdays in the small home where Leonard was born and raised. Early afternoon they could be seen turning the corner on Harrison Street and walking side by side, each with the hand of a child in theirs. The sparkle of love that shone in their eyes had not dimmed as the years passed, and you could tell, just by the way they walked, that their visit was not a duty but a privilege. Up the pavement they walked, waving to Mr. Brown in the corner store, who always stood in the doorway to smile as they passed. Then past the houses of the Richardsons and the Maliskos and the empty lot next to Leonard's mother's home. Every Wednesday was a reunion for Anna.

They would stay pretty much of the day. Anna enjoyed putting together a meal that was a bit larger than she was used to. It was so hard to prepare a meal for only one person. The evening meal was never a feast, but it might as well have been one because of all the love and joy that surrounded the table. When they said Grace on these days, Anna was truly thankful. Then, usually before dark, Leonard, Jeanine, and the twins began their trek home. Leonard still had to get some sleep before going off to take his station as watchman at the local furniture factory.

Just one thing bothered Leonard. He wished he had

enough money to bring his mother a gift when they came to visit. Oh yes, they brought gifts on Christmas and Anna's birthday, but he wanted to do a little more than that. His mother always gave to others. Just once, he wanted to do something special for her. But he could not. It was all he could do to pay the rent, buy the food, and pay for medicine and doctors for the twins when they became ill. Even the clothing they wore had to come from thrift stores because they could not afford new clothing. But no-one really seemed to mind. They had each other, and they were happy. It was just ... well, it would be nice for one time to say a special "thank you" to someone who always gave through her whole life.

One warm August Wednesday, the four turned the corner on Harrison Street. Mr. Brown was waiting in the doorway as usual and smiled warmly as they passed and waved at him. Mrs. Richardson was sitting on her porch rocking vigorously in her rocking chair. Leonard whispered to Jeanine, "She's probably rocking so fast to create a breeze to keep cool." Jeanine gave him a sharp poke in the ribs. "Oh Len," she said, working hard to keep from laughing out loud, "you're terrible."

Mr. Malisko was standing in the shade of the big oak tree in his front lawn. Nearby was his old lawnmower that chewed the grass more than cut it. "Hi Len," he called out. "Sure is a hot one today."

"Sure is," Leonard answered. "It's too hot to be pushing that antique around. Maybe you ought to buy a herd of sheep."

The old man let out a loud laugh and went back to the task of mowing his lawn.

When the family reached the vacant lot, Leonard stopped. The lot was full of wild daisies. The white and yellow shone as brilliantly as the afternoon sun.

"Wait here a moment," he instructed his family. And off he went to pick a large bouquet of flowers.

When he had finished, he returned to his wife and children, and they all continued toward the house on the other side of the lot. The twins ran on ahead, climbed the steps, and shouted through the closed screen door, "Grandma! Grandma, guess who's here!"

"Now who could that be coming to my house today?" she answered as she did every time they came. "Well, my land's sake," she said with pretend surprise, which the twins thought was genuine. "It's Joan and Jason. Come in, come in."

The twins ran into the house, talking at the same time about all of the exciting news they brought. Leonard held the door for Jeanine and gave her a wink as she walked by. "I love you," he whispered and she blushed with the same excitement she experienced every time he said that.

He then went to his mother, kissed her on the cheek, and handed her the daisies from the neighboring field. "Here, mom," he said, "for all of the years of being a true pal and a wonderful mother."

Tears filled Anna's eyes. "Oh Len," she responded, "what a wonderful Christmas gift this is."

Leonard's heart sank. "Is this the beginning of senility?" he asked himself. "How sad it will be to see such a sharp mind destroyed by hardening arteries."

"Mom — " he started to say out loud.

"Len," she said, "I know what you are thinking, and I know that Christmas is in December. I haven't lost all of my faculties, though I do feel as though I am getting slower. But Christmas is not only a season of the year. It is when someone brings the gift of the Christ child into another person's life. That can happen any day of the year, and that is what you have done for me today. Jesus is God's sign of love to his children, and each act of love done in his name is a remembrance of that miracle. These flowers are a gift of love. You have brought something special into my life today. You have made today Christmas for me. I thank you for your love. And because of your gift, I also remember the gift of Christ, the Messiah, the Savior, Immanuel, God with us, the Prince of Peace."

That was a special day. Anna saw the love of her son as a sign that pointed her toward the love of God, which was the source of her hope and strength. Leonard realized that gifts do not have to be bought and that the fistful of flowers he gave his mother was more valuable than a king's ransom. Jeanine felt proud of the man she loved so dearly and knew beyond any doubt that he loved her and that she truly loved him. The twins didn't quite understand why they sang Christmas carols at the supper table that night, but they will never forget how happy everyone was.

There weren't too many more visits to Grandma's house after that. Just a few weeks later, she was taken to the hospital and there her eyes closed peacefully for the last time. It was a time of sadness, surely. But it was also a time of hope. When everyone returned to their cars after the pastor gave the graveside benediction, Leonard, Jeanine, and the twins remained behind and stood side by side, each holding a daisy. One by one, they stooped and placed it on the lid of the casket, remembering a bouquet that had brought a true sense of Christmas into their lives.

It is good to be a gift to others and for others to be gifts to me. But I thank you, Lord, for being our Immanuel. As you are present to me in word, sacrament, and others, so may I, through my surrender to your will, be your presence to others.

The Visit

Theme: loneliness; abandonment; hope
Scripture: Is 61:1-3; Lk 4:18,19; Mt 11:1-15
Feast: third Sunday in Advent (B cycle); third Sunday after the Epiphany (A and C cycles)

Clara was happy. Of course, she was happy every day at this time. This was when her friends came to her house to pay their daily visit. She could count on them; they hardly missed a day. But they never came on weekends. Clara was not happy on weekends. They were so long, and sad, and friendless. She couldn't understand why it was that way, and her friends never told her. "Oh well," Clara said to no-one in particular, "I am so thankful for when they do come."

Sometimes Clara seemed to enjoy her preparations as much as the visit. They had become a ritual for her, and she followed each step in precise sequence. First, she put on her favorite black dress, the one with the white lace collar. She always did look good in that dress. It was old but still very stylish. She looked at herself in the floor-length mirror and admired her thin figure, which she was able to keep these many years.

After dressing, Clara went into the kitchen and put water on the stove to boil for tea. While the water heated, she carried six tea settings into the parlor for her friends. If everyone came, there would be just enough room for them all.

When the cups, spoons, and small napkins were in their proper places, Clara returned to the kitchen, made the tea, and brought the steaming teapot along with some cake or cookies into the parlor. Then she sat down on the maroon-colored mohair divan and waited for her friends to arrive.

Clara knew they would come. They came yesterday; they will come tomorrow. Clara was not surprised, but pleased to see that they were indeed coming again today. She was so glad that this was not a day on the weekend.

She was also very happy to see that they all came today. Their happy voices and faces filled the empty parlor and brightened Clara's spirits.

Bobbie was wearing a new, bright red dress. She looked absolutely radiant. Clara could not get over how good she looked, considering all she had been through lately. Clara was sure that her recent engagement to Sean was the best thing that ever happened to her. She hoped so much to get an invitation to the wedding.

Monica was there as well, obviously pregnant, and so full of life. Clara did hope that Monica was seeing the doctor. "You have to take care of yourself and your baby," Clara advised, hoping that her friend would heed her advice.

All of the visits were pretty much the same. Her friends came. They talked about life, and joy, and tragedy, and hope. Clara listened carefully as they talked among one another. Sometimes she shared some of her own advice when she thought it was called for. It didn't matter all that much if they listened to her. Why should they? Her own children never did, and they never even came by for a visit anymore. Clara was so thankful she had these friends upon whom she could rely — every day except Saturday and Sunday.

Then, as it always happened, Clara's friends had to go.

The visits always ended too soon for Clara. This was a sad moment for her because when they left, there was no-one else. Clara would be all alone, with nobody to talk to, nobody to care. When they went, a good part of Clara's life went also. She knew they had to go. It was just that their visits were over so soon.

When it was time for them to go, Clara got up from her place on the maroon-colored mohair divan and walked over to the other side of the room. "Good-bye," she said to each of them. "Don't forget to come back again tomorrow. I'll be waiting for you. I am so glad you came. Your visit means so much to me. Good-bye."

With one hand she waved, while with the other she reached down and pushed the button on her television set, just as the announcer said, "Tune in again tomorrow for General Hospital ... "

Clara gathered up the cups filled with tepid tea and started to carry them back to the kitchen. "No-one touched the cake today," she said. "Tomorrow, I think I will bake some cookies."

Lord of the visited and the lonely; the mobile and the lame; the sighted and the blind; the hearing and the deaf; the healthy and the diseased; the housed and the homeless; the rich and the poor; the fed and the hungry; the living and the dead — lead me, your servant, and inspire me as those whom you send. Grant that those around me do not have to look beyond but will see in my love and concern your presence in this world today.